Viele, 1659-1909: Two Hundred And Fifty Years With A Dutch Family Of New York

Kathlyne Knickerbocker Viele

VIELE

1659—1909

TWO HUNDRED AND FIFTY YEARS

WITH

A DUTCH FAMILY

OF

NEW YORK

COMPILED BY

KATHLYNE KNICKERBOCKER VIELE

(Graduate of the Woman's Law Class of the University of New York, Member
of New York Genealogical and Biographical Society, Daughters of
Holland Dames, Daughters of the American Revolution, Etc.)

" Gather up the fragments that remain that nothing be lost."

NEW YORK
TOBIAS A. WRIGHT
1909

Kathlyne K. Viele

THE VIELE FAMILY

The name of Viele is first found in the Albany records in the year 1659. There seems to have been no Vieles in New Amsterdam until 1688. In 1659 the name of Aerhnout Cornelisen Viele appears in the Albany record, and two other Vieles, apparently his brothers, Cornelis Cornelisen and Pieter Cornelisen Viele, took up lands in Schenectady,—Cornelis in 1688 and Pieter in 1670. The fact that these bear the name of Cornelisen shows that they were all three sons of a Cornelis. It seems probable of a Cornelis who never came to this country. There were indeed other settlers with that combination of names. In 1644 a Cornelis Cornelisen from Utrecht, age 22, was witness to the burning of a barn in Harlem, and in 1645 in New York is recorded the marriage of a Cornelis Cornelisen j. m. en Aeltje Colet wed; but although both records may refer to the same man it is difficult to point to any circumstance that shows that either referred to a Viele.

Pearson's Early Settlers of Schenectady gives Aerhnout Cornelisen as the son of Cornelis Cornelisen, brother of Pieter Cornelisen, but as Aerhnout is a grandfather apparently before the children of either Cornelis or Pieter are married it would appear absurd to place him in a generation after them. Pearson did wonderfully well in his genealogies, but it was impossible for him not to have occasionally erred, and while his indications are all valuable his deductions cannot always be followed. On the Court Minutes of Albany County in the year 1686 is recorded a complaint against Bennony Arentse v. Hoak, who married Jacomintje Swart, widow of Pieter Cornelisen Viele. This complaint, as it includes mention of all three of the early Vieles,—Aerhnout, Cornelis, and Pieter,—is the only authentic testimony to their mutual relationship. Pieter is dead, his daughter is maltreated by her stepfather, and Cornelis Viele and others enter a complaint; the stepfather is bound over by the court to keep the peace, and the child is put under the guardianship of

Aerhnout Cornelisen Viele and Jacob Meese Vrooman, the stepfather of Jacomintje Swart,—the child's mother. We have here
the facts which show the close relationship between Aerhnout,
Cornelis, and Pieter. In order to arrive at any decision with
regard to the descendants of the early Dutch it is necessary to
bear one or two facts in mind. First, that the early Dutch settlers had seldom a surname. Each individual had his own baptismal name, to which was added his patronymic. As, for
instance, Claas Janse was Claas, son of Jans. To this was sometimes added his trade or the name of the place from which he
came. One of the early Dutch emigrants is identified by his
title,—Jan van Bommel; this distinguishes him from a hundred
other Jans. A second Dutch peculiarity is a most fortunate one
for the genealogist. It was an invariable custom among the
first Dutch settlers to name the children first after their grand-
parents and then after their parents. Along this clue many
genealogical uncertainties may be cleared up. For the first two
or three generations of the Dutch in this country this rule was
closely adhered to. Following this rule the early members of
the Viele family have been placed where they seem to belong.
For the later generations the full marriage and baptismal records
at Albany, Kingston, and New York make the task an easier one.
In Albany the records of the Dutch Church began in 1683. The
massacre of Schenectady, followed as it was by the burning of
the town, wiped out all records preserved there prior to 1690.

Every statement in this little narrative will have its reference given and where proof is not possible to offer, the reason for
making it will be laid before the reader.

While it remains uncertain from whence the Vieles originally
came, indications point in two directions; perhaps they came from
some town of Holland like Wiel in Gelderland or Viel in Lim-
burg or were related to that Laurence van der Wielen, who
came over in the ship "Faith" in the year 1659. My brother,
Herman K. Viele, bought in Amsterdam an engraving of one
Cornelis Staltpart van der Wiel, Doctor of Medicine in the
Hague, "Anno Aetatis Suae LXVII," or "in his sixty-seventh
year," his dress indicating the period of about 1650. This is at
least interesting, as Cornelis Arentsen Viele, son of Aerhnout,
was a practising physician in New York, 1691, and assisted in

aiding those injured in Leisler's rebellion in that year. The other probable origin of the Viele family is from the south of France. Family tradition has always held that the Vieles were French Huguenots, who fled from France to Holland to avoid persecution and became identified with the Dutch. Investigations made lately in Holland throw little light upon the subject; but show that a family named Viel appears first at Amsterdam in March, 1631. No first names of this family identify it with the Vieles of America. A family of Vieles came from France to Holland in 1682 spelling the name Viele. The research was made at Amsterdam, Leyden, Venlo, and the Hague. We must therefore remain in ignorance of the Vieles' early home, or even as to the year that they sailed from it for America, unless armed with a clue that until now is missing. There is at least no testimony to contradict the old family tradition of a French origin which seems not to be confined to one branch but to have gone with the name.

A word about Schenectady, the settlement to which two of the Viele brothers early directed their steps and where the descendants of Cornelis are to be found at the present day. The plantation of Schenectady was first open to settlers in 1662. In that year Arent van Curler and his followers, certain Freedom-loving Dutchmen who had tired of the restraints imposed upon them by the Patroons of Rensselaerwyck, with rare courage, struck out into the wilderness and settled on that lovely spot on the Mohawk, which for years stood as the bulwark between civilization and savagery, and which has ever since remained a city of note and importance.

The Vieles came to Schenectady but a few years after its first settlement, though after the death of the intrepid Van Curler. They purchased their bouweries from the original settlers and afterwards received for them patents from the governor. In these patents the lands are described with the accuracy of present-day deeds. The name Viele in old documents, on marriage and baptismal records is most variably spelt. Such was the case with most Dutch names. The spelling of that day was very unsettled and each chronicler, Domine and official, who added his quota to the records, spelt the name on these records as they sounded to his ear: Viele, Vilen, Vyle, Vile, Vieley, Vely,

Wiele, Wilen, Fil, Fiele, File and even V. Eli, are a few of the names preserved of persons who were undoubtedly Vieles. We who have borne the name in this generation can testify that even now it is a name not only easily misspelled but which it is almost impossible to get spelt correctly. The writer has been impatient when addressed as "Vile," but became somewhat reconciled by finding that "Jacomintje Vile" had a sitting in the Dutch Church in Albany some two hundred years ago. A grievance two hundred years old is a respectable one!

One word as to why this family record has been attempted. My father, Gen. Egbert Ludovicus Viele, spent much time and energy in getting up a family chart which he published in 1775; but there are sources now open for investigation, owing to the widespread interest in genealogy, of which he could not avail himself and by reason of which his family record stands in need of revision. In addition to that my brother, the late Herman Knickerbocker Viele, searched further into the family records with the new light thrown on them, and I myself have spent many hours while recuperating from a severe illness, in the endeavor to know somewhat of those dead and gone ancestors, so that I might present them to their descendants a little as they were in life. Furthermore, my desire was to give general interest to the task by putting on record an average Dutch family which would exemplify the courage, the virtue, the industry, and the power of endurance of those early pioneers who represent the bone and sinew of our national strength. Here are no gentlemen of leisure or dainty dames of fashion; here are the toilers who wrested from the forest and the untilled valleys a hardwon living; here are those who lived in daily expectation of a deadly foe, filled with dread not for themselves but for their wives and little ones, and who endured the agony of seeing, in some cases, their worst fears realized. Here are the women who in the midst of hardships raised large and virtuous families; here are the men and women who failed not to worship God, who cared well for their children, to whom marriage was a life contract, and who lived independent lives on the soil they owned and had dearly paid for. This American family, two hundred and fifty years old in this country, has not lost its strength. Cornelis and Pieter Viele represent successful men for those days, with their large possessions. Most of their lands they seem to have had money to pay for, while the gifts of large tracts of lands from the Indians to Cornelis and Aernhout represent valuable services rendered. Aernhout, the Interpreter, was a man of considerable education (witness his journal) and of much enterprise, energy and determination. He seems to have been much respected both by the English Government and by the Indians of the Five Nations.

In the time of the American Revolution there were more than thirty-five of the family who fought for independence. In one regiment (the Fourteenth Albany Militia) four brothers fought side by side. One Andrew Viele, a soldier of the Line, was at West Point at the time of Arnold's attempted treason and was wounded in the service. Among those who took part on the Union side in the War of the Rebellion were Capt. Eugene Viele, Capt. Charles Viele and my father, Gen. Egbert L. Viele. It was left to my brother to place the Viele name in the ranks of American Literature; to him—

HERMAN KNICKERBOCKER VIELE,

POET AND NOVELIST, AS WELL AS ARTIST OF NO SMALL MERIT,
AND CIVIL ENGINEER OF WORTHY RECORD,
I DEDICATE THIS FAMILY SKETCH.

K. K. V.

VIELE

I

AERHNOUT CORNELISEN VIELE

One picturesque character the family of Viele in this country has produced in the person of Aerhnout Cornelisen Viele, the Interpreter. In the dry details of his life as they are culled in great part from the Colonial records there is depicted a man, adventurous, fearless, untiring, engaged in a task of international interest and historic value. The French and English pioneers eager to acquire the lands of the new world for themselves and their country and small in numbers, soon learned to make use of the Indians in the accomplishment of their purposes. This being the case it was necessary to keep in close touch with the savages and to open up a perfect understanding with them. This could only be done by means of interpreters, and to a knowledge of the languages the interpreters must join a knowledge of the Indian character and of the matter to be negotiated. Evidently beginning as a trader in furs, Aerhnout Viele, in "guide's woolen coat," roamed through the unbroken forest till no place was unfamiliar to him from Long Island to Canada. He apparently began his public career by interpreting deeds from the Indians, next he interpreted official messages at the councils of the Five Nations, and finally he was appointed Provincial Agent or delegate from the Governor. His duties were varied and it will be seen that his whole life was an effort to preserve the Five Nations as a barrier to keep the French above the St. Lawrence. To this end he endured hardships, imprisonment and personal losses, and that he did his work well the records show, and grants of large tracts of land as gifts from the Indians testify to their esteem.

He is the first of the family of whom there is indisputable mention and is by far the best known of the early Vieles.

It is in 1659 that Aerhnout Cornelisen is named as a purchaser at an auction in Albany, and in 1660 some citizens of Albany, among whom is Aerhnout Cornelisen, petition the Council that no Christian brokers be allowed to "roam through the woods," and that only Indian brokers be allowed in the Indian trade.

(Ft. Orange Rec., Vol. XVI., part III., Doc. His. N. Y., and Dutch Mass., p. 323.) A little down the page other citizens make the opposite request of the Council, showing a variety of opinion as to the better policy. In another place the Indians complain that the Dutch agents treated them badly; in fact they accuse them of beating them. Indeed it may well be that the Dutch brokers were obnoxious alike to the Indians and to the traders, for they intimidated the first to get their furs for little, and they, having secured the bargains, sold them for more to the traders than they would have had to give to the Indians directly. Doubtless the Indians were often imposed upon, but it is difficult to pass judgment, as the pioneers, numerically so few, were constantly menaced by undisciplined savage hordes. It is, however, evident that Aerhnout Cornelisen Viele served the Indians well and received from them many marks of their confidence.

Look for a moment at Albany as it was at the time when Arnout first came to it. It was a thriving Dutch trading post, indeed the center of the fur trade. It was still the village of Beverwyck (called also Willemstadt), to which the Indians brought their beavers and other peltries and exchanged them for powder, shot, firearms, tobacco, and, when they could get it, for rum as well. The merchants of Beverwyck also commissioned agents to go through the country to the northern trading stations, of which Oswego was one, to purchase fur for their trade. That Aerhnout acted sometimes in that capacity seems likely from two law suits in which he was defendant in 1691, which will be referred to later on. Whether he acquired his knowledge of the red men in such expeditions or if he also lived among them cannot be known, but he certainly had an intimate acquaintance with them and had become sufficiently well known to the Indians, especially to the Mohawks, to have earned their friendship.

That auction sale in 1659, which appears to be the point where we first come into contact with Aerhnout, was that of Pieterlie Jans, and his purchase was the homely one of "two pewter pans."

At another auction in the same year he bought a "guide's woolen coat." This purchase points to the fact that he started at this time in the business of "boslooper," or trader—for a

husbandman would not need such a coat. (Albany City Rec.
Mun. An., Vol. IV., pp. 247-273.)   In this same year in Albany
Aerhnout signed a paper in the presence of Louwis Kobes, proving
he was at that date of age.   In 1661 another deed was signed
in the presence of Arnout Cor. *Wilen*.   (Mun. An., Vol. IV,
p. 295.)   This form of the name I take to have been the more
correct one and that the name was always pronounced in two
syllables may be due to the fact that it had once a final "n."
On the 17th of March, 1663, Aerhnout Cornelisen Viele purchased
a house and lot at Beverwyck of Jan Costerse van Aecken;
"Done at Ft Orange."   It is likely this was in anticipation of
his marriage to Gerritje Gerritse Vermeulen.   Just when he
married does not appear, but he was certainly married in 1667.
Documents found in old Albany records relating to the efforts
made to procure for her some monies in Amsterdam, Holland,
which were her due give some welcome facts concerning Aerhnout's wife, which will be found in the little account of her further
on.   Their greatest interest for the historian of Aerhnout rests in
the fact that they establish him in 1667 as a citizen of Albany, a
married man, full of a man's responsibilities.   From now on
he will be found taking an active part as trader, interpreter and
landowner; sometimes in capitivity, sometimes roving among the
Indians in the wilds of northern New York, at one time in
Albany, at another in Kingston, Kinderhook or Long Island.
We find him associated as interpreter with the English officials,
with military officers, with the French and English Commissioners and with the Jesuit priests.   And although often placed
in trying circumstances in his position as go-between he retains
to the last his good name with both sides.   Once he was out-
witted perhaps by the Jesuit de Lamberville and the wily French
agents, but he failed not to talk to the Indians in the tone of one,
who expects to be obeyed.   Take him all and all he was a fine
type of the sturdy Dutch pioneers who wrestled so persistently
to secure the lands which are ours to-day.   It was due to such
as he that the French in the North were held in check and our
Empire State was preserved to the English till it became American.   He made an ideal interpreter, for his intimate relations
with the Indians prevented him from cheating them, indeed
incidents occur that show him to have their interest in view,

while the name of "faithful interpreter" given him by the English authorities show that he worked honestly for them.

In 1664 there are two references to him: the first in May, when he is witness to a lease of land from the widow of one of the original proprietors of Schenectady (Wemp.) to Akus Cornelisen (van Slyck), the Schenectady tapster and interpreter. "Done at Rensselaerwyck." (Col. Doc., Vol. XIII, p. 374.) Then in December, 1664, when two pounds of gunpowder are issued to Arien Conely for bringing the Governor's horse. (The same, Vol. II., p. 467.) In 1666 he buys at the auction of Cornelis Bogardus "two little pictures" for 17:oof., one cheese-pot for 3:1of., and a silver becker for 65:oof.—to be paid for in good strong seewant in six weeks' time. (Mun. Col., Vol. III.)—all doubtless for the new home just established.

In 1667 there is a petition of "traders beyond the seas," sent to the States-General in Holland, and one of those who sign it is Arnout van Uhlen (this I take to be intended for "Vilen.")

In 1667 (April 3) the Commissionaries and Magistrates answer to the request of Aerhnout Cornelisen Viele and Storm van der Zee, innkeepers, for a license to keep an Ordinary with monopoly of tapping bier, etc., and on the Court Minutes is recorded that a license was granted to Aerhnout Cornelisen Viele to keep a tavern for travellers. The record does not state whether the Ordinary was to be in Albany or not, but it probably was, and it is a curious fact that he, like Cornelis Cornelisen, should keep a tavern. Wherever it was the care of it must have fallen on his wife, as he was so frequently away. One wonders if he had a business interest in that inn in Schenectady once kept by his brother Cornelis and at the time of the massacre in charge of Douwe Aukes and his wife Maria, Aerhnout's daughter. However that may be, in April of this year (1667), Aerhnout with others hires a herder,—a sign of prosperity. It has been suggested that the fact that the Vieles were such good church members pointed to their Huguenot ancestry and in 1683 when the earliest record of the Dutch Ref. Church is made, Aerhnout and his wife are among the first members. In this year he seems to have given two pieces "of eight" towards the salary of Domine Dellins. For this Arnout was entitled to a seat in the new gallery of the church (the church itself having been built in 1656.)

The first notice of Aerhnout as an interpreter occurs in the English Colonial Mss. (p. 122), in which he is referred to as "Aerhnout Cornelisen, the interpreter." And in the same year (1676) at the Court of Assizes (in New York) William Leveridge was arrested for slandering the Dutch at Albany, fined twenty beavers and allowed six months to make good his charges against Aerhnout Cornelisen, the interpreter." (Brodhead, Vol. II., p. 301.)

In 1675 Aerhnout Cornelisen and Ryer Sanders are sent by the Commissionaries and Magistrates to the Northern Indians at Hoosic to treat for the release of some white prisoners. (Court Minutes.)

On the 8th of August, 1676, Indians report at Albany a meditated invasion by the French. The interpreter was Arnout Cornelisen Viele, who came down with them. (Council Minutes, Albany; Col. His. N. Y., Vol. XIII., p. 499.) January 1, 1677-8, an Indian Deed for land at Claverrick (Ft. Orange Deeds, 3) is done and interpreted by Aerhnout Cornelisen Viele at Albany (signed Aerhnout Cor. Interpreter). Col. Doc. N. Y., Vol. XIII., p. 516.) On March 28, of this same year (1677), an order of Council directs the Mohawks to cease making war on the Eastern Indians. "Order to be delivered in the New Fort by Arnold, the interpreter." (Col. Doc., Vol. XIII, p. 504.)

In 1678 are several items of interest. On May 16, at Albany, Arnout Viele signs papers as juryman in case of the shooting of Indian squaw. (Mun. An., Vol. VIII., p. 171.) On June 11 an Indian Deed for land in Columbia County is done by "Arnout Cornelisen Viele, interpreter." (Ft. Orange Rec., Deed 3.) A letter from Capt. Salisbury to Com. Brockhulst, dated Albany 27 June, 1678, reports the arrival of a party of Mohawks with 22 Natick prisoners "who say they are friends of the English." "Resolved to send yᵉ secretary and Aerhnout the interpreter to yᵉ prisoners to examine them from whence they came, etc." A second letter on July 23, from Capt. Salisbury again, to Com. Brockhulst on Indian affairs, says: "and herewith send Arnout along with them (a company of five on a mission to the Mohawks) into yᵉ land but not to assist them only to go

along to heare what their demand is of the Maqueas yt I may
by the next give you an account of the proceedings, etc." In
the same year Arnout interprets the answer of the Mohawks
to a proposition made them by the Sennecas (Col. Doc., Vol.
XIII., p. 528).

About the same time is a letter from the Commissaries of
Maryland at Albany to Com. Brockhulst telling that the Oneidas
and Onondagas are on the warpath against Maryland "The
Commissarys who readily procured for us five belts of peek to
send to the Five Nations to come to speak with us (which this
morning Arnold went away with)   Since his going we have received informacon yt there are gone two tribes of the Oneidas
down into Maryland and that a third is preparing to go." (same.
p. 55.)

In 1680 Aerhnout received his first gift of land from the Indians which was as follows:

"Indian Deed given by the Indian owners, Kashekan alias Cal-
koen, Waspocheek alias Spek and Philippuwas, having power of
attorney from Awannus, one of the owners to Aerhnout Cornelisen Viele as a present.   The land consists of three flats through
which a kil called Mynachkee runs, one being of about 25 morgans and lying on the northeast side of the kil, the other on the
south side containing altogether about 12 morgans.   The grant
includes the above kil from the river to the second waterfall
called Matapan, a distance of about three English miles to the
north and one mile to the south of the above described land and
back from the river to aforesaid second fall, including two small
kils, one in the woods to the north which empties into the river
and is called Pakakeing the other emptying into the large kil from
the south.   Albany, June 15th, 1680."

This gift is recorded in the Ft. Orange records, but in order to
constitute a clear title it had to be confirmed by a patent from the
governor.   Therefore we find in 1704 Aerhnout Cornelisen Viele
and Peter Lansing pray for patent for tract of land in Dutchess
Co. "on Hudson's River, beginning at a creek called Packeing by
ye river side."   This gift of the Indians to Aerhnout on the
Hudson is referred to in another recorded deed dated 1682.

"Land in Putnam Co., (the county boundaries were doubtless
not well defined), bond and mortgage given by an Indian of the

Highlant for a debt to Laurence van Ale and Gerret Lansing, secured by his land situate upon Hudson's river on the east side
* * * beginning at the second falls where Aerhnout Cornelisen's land ends." (Ft. Orange Records, Notorial Papers,
1677-1695.)

This Indian deed to Aerhnout has won for itself distinction.
It is the first deed for land in Dutchess Co., and was granted
three years before there was any Dutchess Co. It has been of
especial interest as a means of establishing the origin of the name
"Poughkeepsie." I will quote from Platt's History of Poughkeepsie.

"This deed to Arnout dated June 15th, 1680, (Ft. Orange Rec.,
Book 3, Deeds p. 72) three years before there was any Dutchess
Co., is the earliest deed I have found to land within the present
limits of the county. The deed is in Dutch and there are two
translations or abstracts of it which differ somewhat. One is in
Col. His. XIII, p. 545, and the other is in the State Library in
manuscript and contains the important addition that the kil
Wynachkee on which the land lies is 'opposite Danskammer.' The
kil to the woods to the north is here spelt "Pakakeing," which is
the spelling of the Dutch deed—still a perfectly legible document." (Platt's History of Poughkeepsie p. 11-12.)

Aerhnout it appears sold it in 1690 to Pieter Lansing and later,
when the Crown patents were being given out the settlers on
Aerhnout Viele's land, found themselves in danger of losing their
lands since Indian deeds no longer gave a clear title. For this
reason we find him and Pieter Lansing in 1704 praying for a
patent. A copy of the application for this patent is herewith
submitted with the information that the original is in the Secretary of State's office and is in excellent preservation. It is in
English and is in Land Papers, Vol. III, p. 183.

The petition for a patent is as follows:

"To his Excellency, Edward, Viscount Cornbury, Captain
General, Governor in Chief, etc.: The humble petition of Pieter
Lansing and Arnout Cornelisen Viele:—Sheweth That whereas
the above named Pieter Lansing by his petition formerly prayed
a Patent for a certain piece of land in Dutchess Co. lying on Hudson's river, beginning at a Crek called Pacaksing by ye river side

3

running in a straight line three English miles Eastward into the woods thence to Matapan fall thence Westward along ye great kil to Wappingis creek thence along the Hudson's river Northward to Pacaksing creek aforesaid which is the same land which certain Indian proprietors thereof the 15th day of June 1680 gave as a free gift and granted and conveyed the same to ye above named Arnout Cornelisen Viele as more fully appears by a certain writing under ye seal of ye town of Albany taken out of ye records there by ye said Arnout having had leave from Gr. Edmund Andros then at Albany to accept of ye same from ye Indians in consideration of his long and faithful service to ye Government as Indian Interpreter. All which ye said Arnout by his joyning in the signing of this petition does testify and aver to be the truth and hereby acknowledge to have granted and conveyed ye said Peter Lansing for a valuable consideration ye 26 day of June 1690. Your petitioner therefore humbly prays your Excellency will be graciously pleased to grant a patent under his seal of this province to ye said Lansing for ye said lands as above mentioned to his only use and behoof having a great charge of children under a moderate Quit Rent. And in duty bound shall ever pray.

> Pieter Lansing
> Arnout Viele."

This interesting document is endorsed on the back: "Read in Council 15 April, 1704, ordered to ly on the table: 4th May 1704 granted."

On June 26th, 1682, C. van Dyck says:

"Next morning bytimes Aerhnout took horse and proceeded on his journey who, intends with God's assistance to be here again in 20 days time. They (the authorities) have desired him to speak to ye Indians and have them all here at one time."

In consequence of this on August 4th the Commissioners from Maryland and Virginia met the Mohawks, Oneidas and Cayugas at Albany and addressed them on the subject of their breach of treaty by murdering Southern settlers and Indians. Doubtless the same warlike excursion that Aerhnout was sent to ward off but sent too late. This conference was held in the court yard in Albany and the interpreters were Mr. Gerrit van Schlichtenhorst and Aerhnout Cornelisen Viele assisted by Akus Cornelisen, formerly an Indian, (N. Y. Col. MSS. Vol. II, p. 323 et seq.) This Akus Cornelisen is the same van Slyck, a half breed, who was the rival tapster of Schenectady. He is sometimes confused with Aerhnout.

1682, Aug. 14, Aerhnout appointed an assessor of taxes of 100 beavers, 8,800 fl. ($3,250) sworn in.

In 1683 the grateful Indians again gave Aerhnout a tract of land. This time on the Mohawk river above Schenectady. This land was near that of his brother Cornelis and was called Wachkeerhola, after the Indians who had lived there. This grant is in the Albany Deed Book C. 199. In speaking of this deed of land to Aerhnout, MacMurray says: "the above mentioned grant from the Mohawks was that parcel of flat land afterwards called the fourth flat. It is not probable that Viele settled upon it or that his title was regarded as good, for it was about this time occupied by Ludovicus Cobes and his son-in-law Johannes Kleyn under title received from Trustees of the town in 1684. He may have transferred his claim under Indian title to Ludovicus Cobes, scout and secretary. It would require no record as no title had been granted by the governor." (Ludovicus Cobes is referred to elsewhere as brother-in-law to Pieter Cornelisen Viele.)

Here is a translation of the deed of gift to Aerhnout Viele by Mohawk Sachems:

"Before the Commissarys' Court for Albany, Colony Rensselaerwyck, etc. appeared the following Moques Sachems, representing all the three tribes of the Moques, owners of a certain piece of land lyeing about Schenectady on the north side of the river covering about 16 or 17 morgans over against the flat where Jacobus Peck lives called by the Mohawks Wachkeerhola which flat the Mohawks herewith cede, transfer and convey to and for the benefit of Aerhnout Cornelisen Viele Interpreter in consideration of his having great trouble every day with travelling to their land to the Sennekus and to the north and in his other duties among the savages. The transfer is made by them in their quality of lawful owners and proprietors of the aforesaid land and they convey it to Aerhnout Cornelisen his heirs and successors free and uncumbered without burden or tax giving him, Aerhnout Cornelisen his heirs and successors full power and authority, etc.

"Interpreted by Akus Cornelisen at the court house in Albany Sep. 26, 1683."

Dirck Wesselsen
Jan Jansen Bleecker

The mark of Tioskanoenda the turtle.

The mark of Akus
the Interpreter.

The mark of Oweadachave the bear.

The mark of Tahaiadone the wolf.

This deed was signed on Sept. 26th, 1683. Two days before, on Sept. 24th, Aerhnout had come to Albany with messages from the Indians of the West. (Weise's History of Albany pp. 178-9.) Doubtless these three Mohawk chiefs came with him to transfer their land to him before the court. In 1684 the Five Nations having asked Gov. Dongan to place the arms of the Duke of York on their castles as a supposed protection against the French the governor ordered Viele, the interpreter, to place on "each castle as far as Oneigra" the duke's arms. Viele was also told to forbid the Five Nations "as subjects of the Duke of York from holding conferences with the French without permission." (Brodhead, Vol. II, p. 398), and the Senecas were offered 400 cavalry if they would attack the French.

Here is the French report of the matter: "At Onondague Le Moyne met Viele whom Dongan had sent on horseback from Albany to warn the Five Nations not to speak to the French without his permission. Dongan's messenger succeeded very well with the Mohawks at Tiennontoguen and with the Oneidas who promised that they would not go near the French governor. But when Viele came to Onondague he was confronted in a council of that nation and the Oneidas and Cayugas by three French agents much more able than himself. These were de le Barre's messenger, Charles Le Moyne or Acossen—'the partridge'— with the Jesuit father John de Lamberville whom the Iroquois had named Teiornsere—which in their picturesque language meant "the dawning of the day," and his younger brother, James, whom they called Onissante." "But," continues the French narrative, "Dongan's Dutch-English emissary did his work badly. In the Iroquois Council Aerhnout Viele whom they called 'Arie,' spoke 'like a master' to the American owners of New York and told them that they belonged to the King of England and to the Duke of York, that their council fires were lighted at Albany and that they must not talk with the governor of Canada. This discourse offended the Onondagues and they replied that they would go and meet Onnontio. "You say we are subjects of the King of England and the Duke of York, we say we are brethren. We must take care of ourselves. Those arms fixed on the posts without the gate cannot defend us against the arms of De Barre.' " (Brodhead, Vol. II, p. 402.)

This is a French version. As a matter of fact our honest Dutchman did not do his work badly if a bit arbitrarily—for, though opposed by a French diplomat and a clever Jesuit, he kept two tribes in the position he wanted them and on Sept. 10th, 1685, he carried to Gov. Dongan a letter from John de Lamberville, the Jesuit, containing offers of peace. (Mun. Col., Vol. III, p. 43.) It was after this that the Governor bade him beware of the "black gown." These reports do show that the French had somewhat weakened the English influence with the Indians and that they at least have awakened from the illusion that the arms of the Duke of York could ward off trouble.

I would like to quote again from de Lamberville's letters which depict his character. "One Arnaud whom Father Bruyas is well acquainted with came here on horseback from Mr. Dongan to tell the Iroquois that he did not want them to talk with you without permission being complete masters of the land and their conduct towards you, that they belonged to the King of England and the Duke of York, that their council fires were kindled at Albany and he absolutely forbade them from talking to you. When Mr. Charles Le Moine and I shall have the honor to see you we shall give you the particulars of these things and how La Grande Gueule came to high words against this messenger exhorting all the warriors and chiefs not to listen to the words of a man who seemed to be drunk so opposed to all reason was what he uttered."

Now having slandered Aerhnout he ascribes his words to another cause namely:

"It is supposed that Arnaud's visit here to prevent the Iroquois going to see you and to get them to hold a council at Orange (Albany) was an intrique of the Orange merchants who feared that their trade would be diminished by a conference held with you with arms in your hands, for Mr. Dongan had probably departed from Orange when Arnaud left to come here." (Letter from John de Lamberville, missionary at Onondaga to M. de la Barre, July 4, 1684. (Doc. His. of N. Y., Vol. I, p. 87.)

Here is more of de Lamberville's letter to de la Barre concerning the strife between him and Aerhnout for control of the Indians:

"We being two or three days journey from here the messenger produced three belts of Wampum. The first and second are from the Mohawks and Oneidas who have promised Mr. Dongan that they will not meet us here. The third was from the Onnantaques to exhort them to give their wampum belt also for the same thing. This the Onnantaques hesitated to do but wishing to please both sides they pleaded for delay. This," continues de Lamberville, "is a piece of Iroquois cunning not to embroil themselves with Mr. Dongan. Tegannehout acted his part very well and harangued strongly against Mr. Dongan's Messenger in favor of Onnontio. I caress somewhat Tegannehout in order that he may win those of his nation to his opinion and not to suffer them to listen to the solicitations of Sieur Arnaud to whom the Onnantagues have given two wretched belts to say to Mr. Dongan that they could not do other than what he himself urged them to do; to wit to settle matters peaceably with you. * * * Whatever Sieur Arnaud may say we have not neglected to send for the Oneida deputies whom we expect to-morrow."

In Eng. MSS. p. 159, is Akus Cornelisen Viele's report of his mission to the Five Nations in 1684. An item that in Albany in 1685 "Arnout sends his boy on the hill to fetch Indians with beavers," makes the reader wonder if perchance that was where the capitol now stands!

In 1686 Aerhnout received a commission as agent to the court at Lake Onondaga "Gerret Luycasse to hold it till he come."

In this same year he seems to have been a Deputy Sheriff for Albany Co. as this is entered on the minutes of the council: "Presentment by the jury of the County of Albany of Jacobus Kuyler for an assault and battery on Aerhnout Cornelisen, Deputy Sheriff of said county, in the execution of his duty." (Eng. Mass., p. 122.)

In the spring of this year (1686) Aerhnout seems to have gone on an expedition commanded by Col. MacGregorie to act as interpreter. This expedition started from Albany and was for the usual purpose of keeping the Indians friendly with the English, and of preventing conjunction with the French. MacGregorie was especially warned to refrain from in any way "disturbing or interfering with the French." They seem to have been joined by another party under Rooseboom in which were "29 Christians." This last had the misfortune to be captured by the French and their Indians and to be taken captive to Canada (Brodhead, Vol. II, p. 444.) This same fate overtook Aerhnout in the summer of 1687 while he was yet with MacGregorie's command, although at the time he was "going to Ottawa with his party a trading." He was taken prisoner and carried on a French brigatine on "the lake" (Lake Ontario), where he was seen by friendly Indians, and by the Oswego river to Montreal. Apparently he was first confined in Fort Cadarecque, where the prisoners were made to work hard at building, and then taken to Quebec where the prisoners were boarded out for their keep to farmers. (N. Y. Col. Mass., Vol. III, p. 431-432 et seq.). A few years afterwards in 1691 Aerhnout is defendant in two suits which apparently grew out of his position on this expedition. In one of these he pleads guilty, saying: "Since they were taken by the French and robbed of all they had and made slaves in a way, he desired time to pay the same." (Albany City Records, July 14 and August 25, 1691. Mun. An., Vol. II, pp. 238-9.)

While he was still a French prisoner in Canada his friends, the Mohawks, gave up a French prisoner to the family of Viele "to wash the tears of his wife and children." (Brodhead, Vol. II, p. 486.) The Indians did this because, "he hath done good service for us in travelling up and down in our country and we having a French prisoner, according to our custom doe deliver him to the family of Aerhnout in his stead and to wash off the tears of his wife and children.." (Col. Doc. Vol. III, p. 483.)

There is no record of how he escaped from captivity, but on May 28, 1688, Gov. Dongan is instructing him to send the chief of the Five Nations to him and bidding him "beware of the black

gowns." (Eng. Mass, p. 158.) These last were the Jesuit
priests. In January, 1688, Aerhnout writes from Onondaga to
Major Peter Schuyler telling him of his efforts to send Indians
to meet the governor in Albany and to detach them from the
French. (Mun. Col.) In consequence of his endeavors the
Five Nations (1688) warned by "Arie," as they called Aerhnout
Viele, sent delegates to Albany who had a stately interview with
Dongan in the town house. "The next day Dongan named the
Indians 'children' as Andros had done, and told them they need
have no other regard for the French nor hearken to them than
as they are our friends to do them no harm." The conference
ended by Dongan promising to get back for them "their people
who had been taken beyond the seas." (Brodhead, Vol. II, p.
518.) This referred to Indians who had been taken to Europe
and left there.

On June 5, 1688, Aerhnout is at Onondaga keeping the governor informed of what occurs; he writes to Dongan announcing
the arrival of "200 waggones, at Onyagaro," of measles among
the Senecas, of the chief Todobracto who has taken the chief
place among the Senecas, and tells him that the French have set
up a high cross two miles from Niagara. (Eng. Mass., p. 160.)

In 1689 he is again directed to go to Onondaga, and in May of
that year there is recorded the answer sent to the governor from
the Five Nations by Aerhnout Cornelisen, and in July, L. van
Schaick writes to Aerhnout respecting the Indians. (Eng. Mass.,
p. 173.)

On the 25th of December, 1689, there is a letter in Doc. His.,
Vol. II, p. 137, written by Aerhnout Viele to Peter Schuyler and
two days after that, on December 27, an Indian of the tribe of
Ockweese was baptized in the Ref. Ch. at Albany after a public
confession, by the name of Paulus; Paulus was 40 years old and
had been a number of years blind. The interpreters of his confession and also witnesses to his baptism were Aerhnout Cornelisz and Hilletje Cornelisz.

It was also in 1689 that those Frenchmen residing at Stillwater
and Saratoga were brought to Albany on a charge of correspond-
ing with Canada, and one of them—La Fleur—was confined in
the chamber of Aerhnout Cornelisen. (Schuyler's Col. N. Y.,
Vol. III, p. 108.) This incident shows that Aerhnout and his

family are yet residents of Albany. In 1672 he seems to have sold the house he bought in 1663 and to have changed it for a house for which he pays in full, "the last cent with the first." (Mun. Col., Vol. IV, p. 497.) In July, 1692, he sells his house and lot on State street (then called Yonker) Albany, to Anna Cuyler (satisfied by her son Johannes Cuyler, Oct. 16, 1695.) Subsequent events will show that after selling his house he went down to Long Island "to the bay," whether to land he owned there or not it has been impossible to find out.

In 1689 (N. Y. Papers, p. 611), Col. Bayard, writing to Capt. Nicolsen, says: "By our messenger and interpreter, Aerhnout Cornelisen the magistrates here are acquainted with what has occurred to the said Maques Indians."

In January, 1690, a proposition is carried by Aerhnout Cornelisen Viele and Robert Sanders to the Indian general council at Onondaga in behalf of the Albany Convention. (N. Y., Doc. His., Vol. II, p. 137.) Doubtless Aerhnout was up there in the northern part of the state when the Schenectady massacre occurred in February, which was so fatal to his family. It was in this year that Aerhnout was witness to the will of Peter Vosburg, of Kinderhook. (Anjou's Cal. of Wills, p. 446.)

On the 20th of September, 1690, Gov. Leisler appointed him General Agent to reside among the Indians and act according to "his best knowledge, skill and power." (Doc. His., Vol. II, p. 314.)

"By The Lievt. Governor, etc.

Whereas his Majesties Intrest & ye Security of this Province requires in an Espetial manner ye maintenance and Eucourgem^t of ye Contract made (with the five nacons of Indians Concluded at Albany by ye Commissioners May the (3d) 1690 For Corroborating thereof it hath proved very Effectual by employing Mr. Aernout Cornelisse Viele as agent to reside amongst ye sd Indians at their court of Onandage & for ye same purposes I have commissionated Mr. Gerret Luycasse with some others in August last to officiate in such capacity or what might tend unto ye end aforesaid until ye said Aernout should arrive there.

"These are to authorize and appoint you the said Aernout Cornelisse Viele, to be agent for this their Majesties Province of

New York and to go to Onandage & there reside or Continue on such other Parts or Places amongst the said Indians according to Instructions as from time to time you shall receive from the Commissioners at Albany ye Same Strictly to observe & wherein the case shall so happen that notice Cannot be given to them & an answer may be Reasonably Expected from them for your further direction that it is Committed to your Wisdom and Conduct to act and to do acording to ye best of your knowledge, Skill and Power to act and to do in all things becoming such an agent as if you had particular Instruccon & directions from mee or ye said Commissioners which may Conduce to his Majesties Dignity and Interest and to the Security and Advantage of this Province for so doing this shall be to you a Sufficient Warrant & farther you are hereby Empowered to order, direct, apoint, & Controule ye aforesaid Gerret Luycasse & all and every person sent with him or remaining of our people amongst ye said Indians in what shall or may Contribute or tend to ye aforesaid Purposes hereby Willing and requiring all & Every of them to obey your Lawful commands as they wil answer the Contrary at their utmost Perills. Given under my hand and seal at fort William in New York this 20th day of 9br in ye 2nd years of their Majesties Reigne Annoq Dmi 1690."

"About six months after the French lost this fort (Cedaresque) they sent agents to treat with the Indians for peace; of which Gov. Leisler being informed he likewise sent one Mr. Arnold Cornelisen Viele who was his Indian interpreter and in great esteem with the Indians to keep them firm to the English interests, and this Mr. Arnold did so effectively prevail that the Indians seized the French agents, some of whom they destroyed, but the chief, viz.: le Cavalier d'Eau, they sent prisoner to Capt. Leisler who kept him in custody all the time of his government. Under Capt. Ingoldsby's government he escaped into Canada. (Col. Doc., Vol. IX, p. 214.)

Aerhnout retained this post as general agent until after the downfall of Gov. Leisler and then lost his position because he had taken the part of that excellent man.

On Sept. 10, 1691, there is the receipt of Aerhnout to Peter Schuyler for £3 for services on expedition to Canada.

From November, 1691, to March, 1692, there is the record of his having served in a company of fusiliers (Capt. George Bradshaw) "raised by act of assembly to secure ye frontiers at Albany."

"To ye pay of Arnout Cornelise Viele listed ye 3d of November, 1691, to ye 28th of March, 1692, is 196 days at 3d. a day Provisions deducted: £1 16s. 6d." Mark how well a soldier was paid!

It was then because of his experience in the militia that Capt. Arent Schuyler in 1692, when he organized a company of Dutchmen to accompany some Shawanees to their homes, placed it under the command of Aerhnout Cornelisen Viele, "a brave man and one acquainted with the Indian language." (Schuyler's Col. N. Y. Vol. III, p. 186.) He seems to have been absent a long time, and this extract from Schuyler's Colonial New York speaks for itself: "While at Minnisink (Feb. 1693) he (Arent Schuyler) learnt some news of a gratifying character: A few days before his visit three white men and three Shawnees Indians had stopped there on their way to Albany to procure ammunition for Aerhnout Viele, who was on his return with 600 Shawnees Indians, laden with beavers and peltries. Viele had been absent about fifteen months and was not expected home till the next June. This was the first news from him since he left with the Shawnees delegation. He did not arrive as soon as he was expected by the report of his messengers. It was not until August that he reached the Minnisink village and thence proceeded to Kingston where Fletcher met him and gave audience to the Indians. They were in sad plight some having been killed by their enemies who had interfered with the hunting and killed also some of Aerhnout's men."

The Indians in speaking of the time Aerhnout purposed coming home said, "att ye time ye Indian corn is about a foot high." (Vol. IV, p. 98.) After Aerhnout's return from this most arduous expedition he appears to have gone down to Long Island. At any rate he was there in 1698, for when Col. Romer had need of him he speaks of him as "living on the Bay (Wallabout) on Long Island." (Col. Doc., Vol. IV, p. 328.) In 1695, whether officially engaged or not, he seems to have been back at his old patriotic interests, for in February of that year David Jameson reports that he has re-

ceived word through Aerhnout Viele that Count Fronternac has
threatened to fall upon the Onandagas in the spring and has so
told the Sennecas and Cayuguas in secret. The reason he gave
was that Dekanssore broke his word and did not return to Canada. "Dekanssore defys the whole strength of Canada and has
gone to Albany to meet Cayenquieragoe. The whole Five Nations send seven hands of wampum to inform the Mahikanders
or river Indians of this." Aerhnout at the same time (Feb.
1694-5) wrote as follows at the request of the Sachems and captains: "Brother Cayenquiragoe: We expect the enemy daily. Let
us have powder and lead. We do not go to the other side of
the lake to hunt but keep watch lest the enemy surprise us. As
soon as the weather is open we will make our castles stronger.
We desire that you will discharge the selling of rum to any of
our nation. Let our Indians have powder and lead instead of
rum. Let the blacksmith repair our arms for nothing. Ho!
Cayenquiragoe, let us not want ammunition. We have too small
a bag for a beaver. Give order that they be made somewhat
larger, and then we will be satisfied that all is Lyes Onontio hath
said unto us and you do not endeavor our ruin. Let not our
enemies rejoice and laugh at us."

In 1696, on May 11th, Pilworth's report to the English Lords
of Trade relating to matters in New York (N. Y. Col. Mass., Vol.
IV, p. 170) says that the persons "best fitted to treat with the
Indians are Schuyler, late Mayor of Albany, Mr. Dirk Wessels,
Justice of the Peace and Dr. Godefridus, a Dutch minister.
These," he added, "have always treated with them by the help of
one Arnout Cornelis, a poor Englishman who has lived a long
time with the Indians and frequently converses with them."

On Sept. 16th, 1696 (N. Y. Col. Mass., Vol. IV, p 197) the
representatives of Messrs. Gouveneur and Leisler writes to H.
M. Commission of Trade: "Friendly Indians came to Albany to
buy guns and ammunition and many people understood their language, chiefly Arnout Ville who has been their interpreter but
was turned out because he had been concerned in the revolution
concerning Col. Ingolsby." In 1698 on p. 329 of the same record
Col. Romer, writing to Lord Bellemont, says: "I am told that
your Excellency is to come here next month: that being the case
I consider it my duty to propose to you a faithful interpreter—

which will be difficult to be found here and I would dare say not a
faithful one according as I see affairs managed. Therefore, my
Lord, I take the liberty to propose to you a good and faithful interpreter named Arnout Cornelisen Vile, living on the Bay on
Long Island. Dr. Staats will cause him to come to New York
to you that you may be master both of the man and his time."
(Col. Doc., Vol. IV, p. 328.) While this is being written he has
already left the Bay and is employed by the Mohawk Indians to
interpret their complaint against Peter Schuyler, Dr. Godfrey
Dellius, their minister; Mr. Dirk Wessells, and Capt. Evert
Buncker who had used artifice to get their land away by pretend-
ing that it was time of war and it would be best to deed their land
to them. (July 8, 1697.)

On April 7, 1699, the Council and Assembly of New York
direct Captains Schuyler and Bleecker to go to Onondaga and
there leave Jan Baptist and Arnout Viele to watch the Indians
and see that they send nobody to Canada and receive no messages
to induce them to do so. (N. Y. Council Minutes, VIII, Part 2,
II.).

In 1699 there is a journal of Aerhnout's which is recorded in
Doc. His., Vol. IV, p. 560, concerning his negotiations at Onondaga. "I went from N. Y. and came with the boat as far as Kinderhook and there took a canoe and arrived in Albany the 21st
inst. The same day Johannes Glen, Jr., came post from Onan-
dago being sent with the Sachem's express order to see where Jan
Baptist tarried soe long for in nine days the time was expired that
the messengers were to go to Canada, etc." On the 22d
he set out with Captains Schuyler and Bleecker and Jan
Baptist towards the Indian country and details the negotiations
which follow. The journal was written in Dutch originally. On
May 14 Schuyler and Bleecker leave Jan Baptist in Onondaga and
send Aerhnout to New York with two men whom they hire for
thirty shillings apiece. Aerhnout's presence is no longer considered
necessary as the Indians have accepted the governor's proposition
and have agreed to send representatives to Albany on the 23d to
treat (same, p. 562.) In a letter brought by Aerhnout to Bellemont the governor from Schuyler and Bleecker, the words of the
journal are word for word repeated. On p. 564 Aerhnout interprets a long speech made by the chief Dekanssore. Here ends

the public records of as good a public servant as this country has ever had. One gets a glimpse in these dry records of the difficult life of the early settlers with enemies and possible enemies on every side. Constant and unremitting had to be the watch on the "Wilden" capable of such fearful vengeance. None but an intrepid spirit could face them again and again and keep control of them as did Aerhnout Cornelisen Viele.

The last record we find of Aerhnout is in 1704 when he prays for a patent on the land given him twenty-four years before by the Indians. Aerhnout's final resting place is unknown, but his name is perpetuated in the documentary history of four nations, Dutch, French, English and American, and would have been in a fifth if the Iroquois had preserved records.   K. K. V.

GERRITJE GERRITSE VERMEULEN

Gerritje Gerritse Vermeulen was born in Amsterdam, Holland. She was the daughter of Hendrick Gerritse Vermeulen who was in Albany in 1667 at which time he bought a house and lot of Cornelis Vander Burg which he sold the same day to Arent Janse (Timmerman). He must have died soon after this for his widow (whose name does not appear) seems in that same year to be married to Arent Janse-Timmerman (carpenter—that is.) Gerritje seems to have been quite an heiress as appears by the following records which in their dry facts give quite a full account of the wife of Aerhnout Cornelisen Viele. In 1667 Aerhnout Cornelisen Viele, a citizen of Albany, solicits from the Commissioners of Albany, Rensselaerwyck and Schenectady a testimonial to the fact that he is the legal husband and guardian of Gerritje Gerritse born in Amsterdam, Holland. Her stepfather, Arent Janse Timmerman, had tried to obtain from her some monies coming from the Orphan's chamber, but needed further certificate. (Mun. Col., Vol. III, p. 163.)

"By the honorable the commissioners of Albany Colonies of Rensselaerwyck and Schenectady, etc. a certain citizen of this town of Albany in America named Aerhnout Cornelisen Viele appearing before us solicits very earnestly that he may receive a certificate testimonial from us that he was married to one Gerritje Gerritse born in Amsterdam, Holland, which we are unable to refuse him: whereas some years since a power of attorney was given to Harman Vedder also in our jurisdiction dwelling having reference to Arent Janse Timmerman, stepfather of Gerritje Gerritse, in respect to some monies which were coming to her from the Orphan's Chamber but came back fruitless because not especially addressed to the Messrs. Orphan Masters therefore we and all magistrates to whom these presents are served make known the truth to be that the aforesaid Aerhnout Cornelisen Viele is husband and guardian to Gerritje Gerritse, both living and in sound health. Given under our hand and seal in Albany in

America on the 25th of September in the nine and twentieth year
of the reign of our sovereign lord Charles II. by the grace of God
king of Great Britain and Ireland, defender of the faith, Annoy
Dom. 1677."

"Appeared before me, Robert Livingston secratary etc. in the
presence of the honorable magistrates Messrs. Peter P. Schuyler
and Richard Pretty, Aerhnout Cornelisen Viele an inhabitant
here who declared that he appointed and empowered by these
prsents Messrs. Abraham de Hoshipel and Daniel de Nieville,
merchants dwelling in the city of Amsterdam specially to demand,
to ask and to receive from the Messrs. Orphan Masters of the
same city the sum of 250 Carolus guilders with the interest due
on the same since the 24 of Aug. 1656, to the date of payment
arising out of the proven estate of the subscriber's wife and by
virtue of an authentic copy herewith given of a certain extract
from the 25th register of the Orphan's Chamber of the city of
Amsterdam Vol. III, drawer 289, etc."

"Appeared before us undersigned Commissioners of Albany, etc.
Arent Janse, master carpenter, here, proposing to return to Holland who declares that in consequence of the sentence of the
Court of date the 18-20 of June and 25th of June-July of this
year by the honorable court here he gives a special mortgage bond
on his house and lot standing and lying here in Albany as the lot
was received by him from Hendrick Gerritse Vermeulen of date
the 23-4 April, May (1667), free and unincumbered, save the
lord's right together with what was conveyed to him by the death
of his Godmother Lisbet Willemse in the custody of his brother,
Wm. Janse * * * at Amsterdam in Holland, and further
more generally his person and estate, personal and real nothing
excepted, subject to all laws and judges to receive them without
loss or cost in case it be found at Amsterdam that he the subscriber, is obliged to distribute (pay out) the 200 and 300 guilders in the sentence mentioned with the interest thereon to the
estate of the father of Gerritje Gerritse, wife of Aerhnout Cornelisen (Viele), also dwelling here but if the contrary be true
according to the allegation of the subscriber then according to
the tenure of the aforesaid sentence this mortgage deed is
to be void and of no effect. D. V. Schellugne, 1668." On
September 3-13, 1668, Aerhnout Cornelisen Viele is granted per-

mission by the Albany Council to sell at auction a cellar of Arent
Jansen on which he holds a mortgage. (Council Minutes,
1668-72.)

AERHNOUT CORNELISEN VIELE, first heard of in Albany in 1659,
and last heard of in Dutchess Co. 1704, m. Gerritje Gerritse
Vermeulen from Amsterdam, before 1667. Children:

+4   Maria Aroutse, m. 1st sometime before 1684, Mathys
      Vrooman, of Albany; 2d, Feb. 4, 1685, Douwe
      Aukes, of Schenectady. Killed with her two
      children at the massacre of Schenectady in 1690.

+5   Willemje, m. 1st Symon Schermerhorn; 2d, Levinus
      Winne, June 20, 1699; 3d, Johannus Van Hoesen,
      June 19, 1709.

+6   Cornelis Arentsen, m. 1st, Maria Aloff, Sep. 28,
      1688, in New York; 2d, Catharina Bogardus,
      April 23. 1693, in New York.

+7   Jacomintje, m. Abraham Abrahamsen in New York,
      Jan. 1, 1692.

+8   Gerrit, m. Janneken Hendrix van Feurden May 24,
      1693, in New York.

+9   Aerhnout, Jr., m. Elizabeth Hendrix van Feurden
      before 1705, in which year he seems to have died.

+10   Philip, m. Antje Louw, July 20, 1701, at Kingston,
      and died in 1761.

+11   Susannah, m. Johannes Wendell June 5, 1708.

4

MARIA AROUTSE[2] VIELE, of Aerhnout Cornelisen[1],
m. 1st Mathys Vrooman of Albany; 2d Douwe Aukes of
Schenectady; children (Vrooman):

  12   Geertruy, b. before 1684.

Children (Aukes):

  13   Margriet, bap. Mar. 21, 1686.

In Mun. Col., Vol. IV, p. 85, is the entry: "1684, Maria
Aroutse Viele." At this time she was married and the mother

of at least one child; for Pearson has this record: "Peter
Merse Vrooman settled in Beverwyck near the church
in 1677. His son Mathys made with his wife, Maria Aroutse
Viele a joint will in 1684 in which there is mention of one
child, Geertruy." Mathys Vrooman did not long survive the
making of this will, for in 1685 his widow seems to have married Douwe Aukes, an associate of her uncle Cornelis (and
doubtless also of her father, Aerhnout, who was also an innkeeper) in the conduct of his Ordinary in Schenectady. On
March 21, 1686, is recorded in the Dutch Ref. Church in Albany the baptism of "Margriet, parent Douv Aukes: witnesses:
Willemje Schermerhorn, Aerhnout Vile & Symon Schermerhorn." (It was not until 1691 that the mother's name was
added to baptismal records.) The history of Maria Viele
Aukes is a brief and sad one. She and her two children—
probably this little Margeriet and the older Geertruy, were
killed at the Schenectady massacre.

DOUWE AUKES (DE FRESSE),

came to this country in 1663 on the ship "Stettyn" from Arn-
heim when 24 years old. He early settled in Schenectady as
an innkeeper or "vicctaller," and was associated with Cornelis
and probably also with Aerhnout Viele. On Feb. 4, 1685,
the Albany church records "Douve Aukens j. m. of Schenectady and Maria Viele, wed. of Mathys Vrooman of New Al-
banian." (Holland Soc. Year Book, 1905.) Another record
reads: "Maria Viele, wife of Douv Aukens and her two children kild 3, And his negro woman, Francina, 1, Maria Alolf
wife of Cornelia Viele shott, 1:" These five persons were
killed in one house standing on the south corner of Mill Lane
and State street next to the ancient church. (Doc. History of
N. Y., Vol. I, p. 304.)

On Dec. 28, 1689, Douw Aukens was commissioned Justice
in Schenectady, and in 1690, on Oct. 8, he was commissioned
Ensign in Albany. Both of these commissions were by Gov.
Leisler. (Doc. His. of N. Y.).

In 1698 Aukes is a witness at the baptism of the child of
Debora Viele and Daniel Kettelkuyn who named two children
after him. In 1697 he is described as "head of the family."

Pearson says: "His (Cornelis Cornelisen Viele) granddaughter's husband, Douv Aukes, succeeded him as innkeeper, and as he grew older he made his wife's *uncle,* Cornelis Viele, Jr., the keeper of his inn." Also further on Pearson continues: "In 1719 when 80 years old, Douv Aukes conveyed to Cornelis Viele, son of the former owner and keeper of his inn, and *uncle* of his late wife, Maria Aroutse Viele, whom he called his son, all his estate in the village (Schenectady).

This is correct excepting as to the relationships, since the proof is strong that Maria Aroutse, dau. of Aerhnout, must be the cousin, not the niece of Cornelis Viele, Jr., son of Cornelis Viele,, the first settler.

MacMurray says that the land conveyed by Douv Aukes to Cornelis Viele, Jr., was as follows:

"1. One house and lot where he (Aukes) dwells,

2. One other lot of—and barn behind or on the West of lot aforesaid near to the grist mill that belongs to ye church (Dutch Church).

3. One other lot of pasture ground on the south or West side of the crek whereon said mill stands.

4. One other lot of pasture ground lying off the east side of the street that leads directly up to the first gate (Ferry street) near to the fort." (Old deed.)

Pearson says: "Benjamin Robert owned a farm at Maalwyck, west of Viele's, also the land opposite on the south side of the river, called Poversons, which he sold to Hend. Lamb Bont, and Bont to Viele, of which said lands were confirmed by patent of date of Sep. 29, 1677—and by Bont's son to Douwe Aukes, who conveyed the same to his adopted son, Cornelis Viele, junior, son of the first Cornelis."

On Oct. 11, 1699, the oath was administered to Douve Auckels, and in 1720 his name appears as a freeholder in Schenectady. *Domine* Aukes who signs as witness to the will of Carel Hansen Toll, is doubtless Douv Aukes. (Ulster Co. Wills, Vol. I, p. 74.)

On Nov. 3, 1733, Doww Aakus, of Schenectady, having died intestate, Letters of Administration were granted to Cornelis Fieling, of same place. (N. Y. His. Soc. Abt. of Wills, Vol. III, p. 126.)

Douv Aukes must not be dismissed without a word of comment. He took the somewhat unusual step of adopting as his heir one alien to his blood. Rendered by that dreadful massacre of 1690 wifeless and childless he finds in Cornelis Viele, Jr., a valued assistant and no doubt affectionate relative. The curious name of Douv Aukes appealed to the imagination of my brother, Herman Knickerbocker Viele, and he has introduced him in a fanciful way into his book "The Last of the Knickerbockers."

5

WILLEMJE[2] VIELE, of Aerhnout Cornelisen,[1]
m. 1st, Symon Jacobs Schermerhorn; 2d, Levinus Winne, June 20, 1699; 3d, Johannes van Hoesen, June 19, 1709. Children (Schermerhorn):

14 Johannes, b. 1684.
15 Aernhout, b. 1686; m. Marytje Beekman Oct. 14, 1713.
16 Maria, b. 1693.
17 Jannetje, b. 1695.

Children (Winne):

18 Maria, b. 1700.
19 Sara, b. 1702.
20 Benjamin, b. 1706.

Symon Jacobs Schermerhorn was the son of Jacob Jansen Schermerhorn, who came over to this country about 1642, and Jannetje, dau. of Cornelis Segars, his wife. When Jacob Schermerhorn made his will in 1688 he mentioned his son as residing in Albany, but in 1690, when Schenectady was burnt he was a resident of that village. Dr. W. W. Battershall, of Albany, wishing to give a picture of those troublous times writes: "We get a glimpse of the situation and of the current history in the scene on that Sunday morning the 9th of Feb., four years after the granting of the charter (1690) when Symon Schermerhorn, shot through the thigh, told at the northern gate of the stockade his breathless story of the night attack

and the horrible massacre at Schenectady." A tablet on the
wall of a house in Albany opposite the railway station com-
memorates this incident. On that fatal night was "killed ye
sonne of Symon Schermerhorn and three negroes of Symon
Schermerhorn's." Albany did what she could to help the suf-
ferers and aid was given through the Deacon Johannes de Wandelaer. Schermerhorn came in for one pair of hose and 6¾
ells sarge: also 70 ells of "Osenburg" linen.

In 1693 Symon was a skipper on the Hudson River. He
must have died before 1696 for his widow in that year married Levinus Winne. Levinus was the son of Peter Winne,
who came from Ghent, Flanders. (Will 1684.) Levinus was
the widower of Teutje Martens when he married Willemje
Viele. ("June 20, 1699, Levinus Winne wedr. of Teuntje Martens and Willemje Viele, wid. of Symon Schermerhorn, both
living here. Married in Albany by Johannes Schuyler, Justice.") Levinus Winne is mentioned among the inhabitants
of Albany in 1720. (Col. His. N. Y., Vol. IX, p. 754.)

Johannes van Hoesen, of Kinderhook, was the son of Jan
Jansen van Hoesen, of Kinderhook, whose father, Jan Franse
van Hoesen, came to Beverwyck in 1646. Jan Jansen van
Hoesen removed to Kinderhook where his family remained for
seven generations, keeping long to the habits and language of
their forefathers and living long lives content with their lot
and masters of the soil on which they lived. (Mun. Col., Vol.
I, p. 76.)

6

CORNELIS ARENTSEN[2] VIELE, of Aerhnout Cornelisen[1],
m. 1st, Maria Alolf, Sep. 28, 1688; 2d, Catharina Bogardus,
April 23, 1693. Children:

21 Volkert, b. 1689; wit. Aerhnout Viele and Ariaantje
Wendel (Albany Dutch Ch. Rec.).
22 Sara, b. Apr. 24, 1695.
23 Gerritje, b. Jan. 3, 1697, m. Joseph Makepees.
24 Cornelis, b. 1702.
25 Cornelia, m. Francis Childe in 1717 (probably belongs here.)

"1688, Sep. 29, Cornelis Arentsen Viele, van N. Albanien
j. m. en. Maria Alolf, j. d. van N. Y." (N. Y. Mar. Vol. I,
p. 65.)

1689-90. On a "List of ye people kild and destroyed by ye
French of Canada and their Indians at Shinnech-
tody 20 miles to ye Westward of Albany btween Saturday and
Sunday ye ninth day of February 1689-90" appears the name
of "Maria, wife of Cornelis Viele shott."

1689-90. The Albany City Records state: "Att a meeting
of ye convention of Albany ye 15th day of February 1689-90
present Peter Schuyler, Mayor, etc—Resolved to write to ye
governor and Council of Boston, Connecticut and Virginia and
to ye civill and military officers of New Yorke and desyre them
to joyn together that Quebec may be taken in the spring as per
letters appears:—Stephn Lee and Mr. Davenport to go by post
to Boston and Cornelis Viele to New York." (Mun. An., Vol.
II, p. 320.)

1691. Cornelis Viele in New York stands sponsor to the
child of Peter Adolfsen (probably his brother-in-law.)

1691. There is the record in Albany of "A list of persons
departed from Albany without any leave or giving notice:
"Laurens, alias Koehaerder, Jan Laurens, Cornelis Laurens, N.
B. Cornelis Viele Surgeon to send up Jan Janse, Everet Wendel, Jr., Symon Schermerhorn, for our want of him is great,
Myndert Hermanse, and Abraham Kip." Which seems to
mean that the Laurens with all the aliases must be searched
for by Cornelis Viele and that he must send back the others
who have gone to N. Y. without leave.

1692, March 24. (This item is preserved from the papers
of Govs. Ingolsby and Fletcher.) "Petition of Cornelis Viele
for payment of his accounts for surgical attendance on divers
persons wounded in Leisler's late rebellion." (Eng. Mass.,
p. 222.)

1692. Inventory of estate of P. Smith taken in New York,
Dec. 23, includes "A ledger book beginning with Albert Bosch
and ending with Cornelis Vieller." (Abst. of N. Y. Wills, Vol.
I, p. 218.)

1693. "den April 23, Mr. Cornelis Viele wedi van Maria Adolfs en Catharina Bogardus j. d. van N. Y. getruwt mit een lisentie." (N. Y. Mar.)

1696. May 29, Cornelis Viele appointed executor of a Will in N. Y. dated June, 1696, proved before Lord Cornbury, 1704.

1698. Cornelis Viele is listed as practising Surgeon in N. Y.

1701. Cornelis Viele in N. Y. signs a petition to William III. from the Protestants of N. Y.

1702. Cornelis Viele executor (with Gerrit) of a Will in N. Y. dated Sep. 14, 1702.

1703. Cornelis van Vielen is among the taxable citizens of N. Y. (2. m. 1. f., 3 children, 1 negro child.)

Although Pearson names but one son of Aerhnout, Cornelis Arentsen Viele, Surgeon, is undoubtedly his son; the internal evidence will bear this out. He stands frequently as sponsor for the children of his brother and sisters as well as for outsiders.

Catharina Bogardus, whom he married, doubtless belonged to the family of Everhardus Bogardus and Jannake Jans, the former owners of the Trinity Church property. Everhardus Bogardus and Blandina Bogardus, grandchildren of these first, stand godparents for the children of Cornelis and Catharina and they return the compliment.

There is the record of the marriage of a Sara Viele in N. Y. to James Marcke (child Barnardus 1713), but as Gerret Viele also had a daughter Sara it is impossible to say which m. Marcke. Both Saras were born in 1695.

7

JACOMINTJE[2] VIELE, of Aerhnout Cornelisen[1],
m. Abraham Abrahamsen, Jan. 1, 1692. Children (Abrahamsen):

26 Abraham, b. 1692.
27 Arnout, b. 1694.
28 Francyntje, b. 1698.
29 Andries, b. 1702.

Jacomintje has been recorded as a daughter of Aerhnout first
because Aerhnout's wife stands for her little Aerhnout together with her son Gerrit. Aerhnout Cornelisen himself
probably being away at this time on a mission to Onondaga.
Second, because Jacomintje names her first son after his own
father and father's father, and her second son after her own
father, Aerhnout; it will also be observed that the sponsors
for her children are Vieles of the Aerhnout Viele branch.
These sponsors are as follows:: Cornelis Viele, Wilemje Viele,
Gerrit Vile and Gerritje Vile, Catharina Bogardus, wife of Cornelis Fiele, and Susanna Viele.

"Abraham Abrahamsen j. m. van N. Yorck en Jacomintje
Vilen j. d. van N. Albanien beyde wonende all hier 1692 1st
January."

8

GERRIT[2] VIELE, of Aerhnout Cornelisen[1],
    m. Janneken Hendrix van Feurden, May 24, 1693. Buried
May 27, 1730. Children:

    30 Sara, b. 1695.
    31 Aerhnout, b. Apr. 25, 1697; m. Zara Pierson Feb.
            13, 1732; buried in N. Y. 1754.
    32 Margrieta, b. Aug. 3, 1701.
    33 Hendrick, b. 1702 (twin).
    34 Jannetje, b. 1702 (twin); baptized in the Dutch
            Church in New York.
    35 Maria, b. Dec. 3, 1704; m. Lewi Theibou Jan. 22,
            1729.
    36 Margriet, b. 1707.
    37 Elizabeth, b. 1709.
    38 Abram, b. 1712.

1693, "Gerrit Vielen j. m. van—en Janneken Hendrix van
Feurden j. d. van Nieuw Yorck beyde woonede alhier. den 24
May mit een lisentie." This is a son of Aerhnout Cornelisen
Viele and Gerritje, named after her father, Hendrick Gerritse.
His first child is named after his wife's mother, Sara van
Feurden and his eldest son is named Aerhnout after his father.

1700. Gerrit Viele stands witness for Gerrit, ch. of Abraham Abrahamsen and Jacomintje Viele.

1701. Witness to Catharina ch. of Cornelis and Catharina Viele (other witness Blandina Bogardus.)

1702. Witness to Cornelis, ch. of Cornelis Viele and Catharina Bogardus. (Other witness, Jaccmintje Viele.)

1702. Gerrit Viele named as executor of will in N. Y.

1703. May 25, Gerrit Viele, one of the appraisers of the estate of T. Van Borsum (Abt. of Wills, His. Soc., Vol. I, p. 314.)

1705. Witness for Sara, dau. of Aernhout Viele, and Elisabet V. Feurden (other witness, van Feurde. Wed.)

1709. Gerrit Viele, witness to a Will in N. Y.

1710. Gerrit Viele is witness to a Will in N. Y.

1711. Gerrit Viele has a commission to enlist the Indians on Long Island.

1711. Witness for Gerrit, son of Philip Viele and Antje Louw (Kingston, N. Y.).

1719. Pet. Gerrit Viele of N. Y. to be appointed sealer of weights and measures.

1720. Witness for ch. of Francis Childe and Cornelia Viele (other witness Catharina Viele (Bogardus.)

1722. Gerret Viele makes deposition. "Gerret Viele, brasier." (Eng. Mass., p. 473.)

1737. Jannetje Viele buried from Dutch Church in N. Y.

9

AERHNOUT VIELE[2], JR., of Aerhnout Cornelisen[1],
m. Elizabeth Hendrix van Feurden. "Overleden" in 1705.
Children:

39 Sara, b. 1705.

Aerhnout Viele, Jr., was carried off by the French from Schenectady on that night of February, 1689-90, so fatal to his family, and held in captivity for three years. He was one of the small band of "27 men and boys" who were led captive from the burning town after seeing their friends mas-

6

sacred and their homes destroyed. From the colonial report
of his escape he must still have been but a youth. "Upon
which we marched about two miles when a Christian boy,
Aerhnout, the interpreter's son, came to us who had been
three years a prisoner among the French." (Mun. Col., Vol.
III, p. 70.) It is there stated that he also was an Indian interpreter. (Col. Doc., Vol. IV, p. 17) to which is added that he
made his escape upon the "occasion of the attack upon the
Mohawk castles by the French in 1693." The word "overleden" after the name of Aerhnout in the record of his daughter Sara's baptism seems to prove that he was dead at that
time. The witnesses were Aerhnout Viele and Gerritje his
wife. (Kingston Ch. Rec.).

Pierson calls her Elizabeth Hendricks, but the Kingston
records call her van Feurden. She is evidently sister to the
wife of Gerrit Viele of New York, Jannetje Hendrix van Feurden. Sara is doubtless named after her mother's mother,
Sara van Feurden.

The will of Elizabeth Viellet, Wid. of New York (Surrogate's office, N. Y. Oct. 13, 1752) leaves all her estate to her
cousins, Andriese Abrahamse and Adriantie Seymour "intrust
for my daughter, Sarah Vielle, for her maintainance during life,
and after her death & after paying the expenses of her decent
interment, I leave to my said cousins all my plate and jewels,
etc. (proved Oct. 27, 1752).

10

PHILIP[2] VIELE, of Aerhnout Cornelisen[1],
  m. Antje Louw of New York, July 20, 1701. (Kingston Ch.
  Rec.). Children:

> +40 Petrus, b. July 5, 1702, m. Elizabeth Louw Aug.
>   14, 1731.
> +41 Aerhnout, b. July 1, 1704, m. Catrina van Keuren.
> +42 Philippus, b. ———, m. Helena Burhans Mar. 2,
>   1731. (In will of Joh. Burhans of Kingston,
>   1758, mention is made that his second child,
>   Magdelina (Helena) bap. in Kingston Apr. 6,

1707, m. Mar. 21, 1736, Philippus Viele, Jr. (Anjou's Ulster Co Wills, Vol II, p. 31.) In 1761 d. Daniel Burhans, Jr., of Brabant. Kingston, who mentions in his will his sister Helena who m. Philip Vielen. (His. Sec. Wills, Vol. VI, p. 97.) 1743-4 Philip Nele (Viele), Jr., executor of will of his brother-in-law, Wm. Legg, Jr. (His. Soc. Wills, Vol IV, p. 57.) Wilhelmus Burhans, Helena's brother, m. Wm. Legg's sister Margaret).

+43 Cornelius, b. ——, m. Elizabeth Louw, Oct. 10, 1734.

+44 Gerrit, b. Sep. 8, 1711, m. Catharina Bratt Dec. 24, 1746.

+45 Johannes, b. Oct. 9, 1715, m. Cornelia Catharine Vanderburg Dec. 7, 1751.

(Will of Gysbert Vanderburg, of Kingston, dated 15, July, 1755, "I leave to my daughter, Cornelia Catharine, wife of Johannes Viele during her life my orchard lying a little to the southward of Kingston"—"I make my three sons-in-law Joh. Vielle (and others) my executors." (Translated from the original low Dutch). (His. Soc. Wills, Vol. VIII, p. 98.) 1738. Johannes Viele, member of Foot Co. of Militia of the Cor. of Kingston, Ulster Co. (Capt. Tjerck de Witt.) (Doc. His. N. Y., Vol. IV, p. 229.) 1745. John Viele wit. to will of Gilbert Livingston of Kingston. (N. Y. Gen. Rec., Vol. I, p. 128).

+46 Maria, b. 1724, m. Cornelis Wynantse Vanderburg Apr. 13, 1751.

+47 Helena, b. 1727, m. Mattys van Keuren July 10, 1746. (All from Kingston Ch. Rec.).

There have been many Vieles in Dutchess Co. and most of them can be traced as descendants of Philip Viele. It seemed a problem to discover from which of the early Vieles Philip had descended. He named his first son Peter and yet it was recorded in an old Schenectady deed that in 1699 Louwis Viele was the "only surviving son" of Pieter Cornelisen Viele. The clue of naming the child after its grandparent seemed to have failed until it was found that Pieter was the name of the child's maternal grandfather—Pieter Cornelisen Louw. The next son was named Aerhnout, and Aerhnout Cornelisen Viele and his wife stand as witnesses at his baptism. Philip in his marriage notice is described as from Albany. All this points to Philip as a son of Aerhnout Cornelisen Viele.

Antje Louw was the daughter of Pieter Cornelisen Louw who came from Holstein Feb. 1659, in the ship "Faith," and married in 1668 Elizabeth, dau. of Mattys Blanchan, and had issue: 1, Cornelis, 1670; 2, Madalina (Helena), and 3, Antje, m. July 20, 1701, to Philip Viele, b. in Albany, and seven other children. (Mun. Col., Vol. I, p. 35).

Philip Viele's will as recorded at Kingston, N. Y., is as follows:

"In the name of God, Amen. The 24th day of March in the year of   Christ 1758. I, Philip Vielee of the town of Kingston in the county of Ulster and the Province of New York, being weak of body but of Perfect Mind and Memory,— thanks be given therefor unto God—Calling unto Mind the Mortality of my body and knowing well that it is appointed unto all Men once to die, do make and Ordain this my last will and testament in manner following—that is to say, Principal and first of all I give and Recommend my soul into the Hands of Almighty God that gave it and my Body I recommend it to be buried in a Christian-like Decent Burial at the Discretion of my executors nothing Doubting but at the General Resurrection I shall receive the same again by the Almighty Power of God that gave it me and as touching such Worldly Estate wherewith it has pleased God to bless men with in this life,— I give, devise and Dispose of the same in manner following:

First—It is my will and I do order that all my Just debts and funeral Charges Shall be paid in A Reasonable time after my Decease.

Secondly—I give unto my Grandson, Cornelius Vielee, son of my son Petrus Vielee, a large Dutch Bible which is in the Possession of his Mother Elizabeth Vielee as for his birthright being in lieu of any thing he might claim as his birthright.

Thirdly—I give and bequeath unto my daughter, Helena, and to her heirs and Assigns forever my Large Looking Glass and see horses thereunto belonging.

Fourthly—I give and bequeath unto my son Aernhoud Vielee and to his Heirs and Assigns forever the Just eighth part of all my estate both Real and Personal wherever the same may be found.

Fifthly—I give and bequeath unto my son, Philip Vielee, Jr., and to his Heirs and Assigns forever the Just eighth part of all my Estate both Real and Personal what soever (wheresoever) the same may be found.

Sixthly—I give and bequeath unto my son, Cornelius Vielee and to his Heirs and Assigns forever the Just eighth part of all my estate both Real and Personal whatsoever the same may be found.

Seventhly—I give and bequeath unto my son, Gerrit Vielee and to his Heirs and Assigns forever the Just eighth part of all my Estate both Real and Personal wheresoever the same may be found.

Eighthly—I give and bequeath unto my son, Johannes Vielee and to his Heirs and Assigns forever a Just eighth part of all my Estate both Real and Personal wheresoever the same may be found.

Ninthly—I give & bequeath unto my daughter, Helena, wife of Mathew v. Keuren, to her Heirs and Assigns forever the Just eighth part of my Estate both Real and Personal wheresoever the same may be found.

Tenthly—I give and bequeath unto my daughter Maria, wife of Cornelius Vanderburgh, and to her Heirs and Assigns forever the Just eighth part of all my Estate both Real and Personal wheresoever the same may be found.

Eleventhly—I give and bequeath unto the Heirs and Devisors of my son, Petrus Vielee Deceased the Just eighth part of all my Estate both Real and Personal wheresoever the same may be found, my executors hereafter named first paying out of the same two certain bonds or obligations for which I am become bound unto the Ministers, Elders and Deacons of the Reformed Dutch Church of Kingston together with the interest due on the same, which is for the Proper Debt of my said

son, Petrus Vielee Deceased, hereby empowering my executors
hereinafter named to pay the same bonds or obligations and Interest as aforesaid out of the said Just eighth part of my Real
and Personal Estate which I have bequeathed unto the Heirs
and Devisors of my said son, Petrus, Deceased.

Twelfthly—It is my will and I do Order that if any of my
above-named children shall happen to die without Lawfull
Issue that then such share or shares shall be equally divided between the surviving children, share and share alike.

Thirteenthly—I give and bequeath unto my Dear and well-
beloved wife, Antje after the payment of my Just Debts the
full Income and Disposition of All my Real and Personal Estate during her Natural Life-time.

And lastly I do appoint Executors of this my last will and
Testament, My Dear and well-beloved wife, Antje and sons
Philip Viele, Jr., and Johannes Vielee for to fulfil and perform
this my last will.

    Signed   PHILIP VIELEE.
Witnesse:

Johannes Jansen,
Christopher Tappan,
D. Wynkoop, Jr.   Proved March, 5th, 1761.

II

SUSANNA[2] VIELE, of Aerhnout Cornelisen[1],
    m. Johannes Wendell June 5, 1708 (John, Wendell, bap. June
13, 1684, buried Oct. 21, 1743). "June 5, 1708, with license,
Johannes Wendell, son of Hieronymous, j. m. and Susanna
Viele, j. d. both born and living in Albany." (Holland Society
Year Book, 1905). Children (Wendell):

  48   Arriaantje, b. Mar. 6, 1709-10, wit: Harmanus
         (Hieronymous) and Arriaantje Wendell.
  49   Gerritje, b. Apr. 17, 1711, d. y.
  49a Gerritje, b. May 6, 1712.
  49b Elsie, b. Feb. 12, 1715-16.
  50   Johannes, b. Jan. 26, 1719-20, m. Sarah Bergen Sep.
         20, 1750. (Talcott's N. Y. and N. E. Fam., p.
         389.)

1702. Susanna Viele stands witness to child of Gerrit Viele in New York, and to child of Jacomintje Viele (Abrahamsen).

25

CORNELIA[3] VIELE, of Cornelis,[2] Aerhnout Cornelisen[1], m. Francis Childe in 1717. Children:

51 Cornelis, b. Oct. 16, 1720.
52 Catharina, b. 1722.
53 Francis, b. 1724.
54 Elizabeth, b. Oct. 12, 1726.
55 Cornelia, b. Oct. 9, 1730.
56 Anna Maria, b. 1739.

Cornelia Viele "huys vrow" of Francis Childe has been assigned as daughter of Cornelis Viele and Catharina Bogardus because of the name of her children and the names of their witnesses, Gerrit Viele, Catharina Viele, Jacomintje Abramsen (Viele), Aerhnout Viele and Catharina Viele again.

1732. Francis Child, member of N. Y. Militia (Capt. Stuyvesant's Co.).

35

MARIA[3] VIELE, of Gerrit,[2] Aerhnout Cornelisen[1], m. Lewi Theibou, Jan. 22, 1729. Children (Theibou):

57 Maria, b. 1733.
58 Lewis, b. ——.

Witnesses to baptism of these children, Aerhnout Viele, Sara Viele j. d., Jannetje Viele j. d. (Note that Sara and Jannetje at this time (1733) are still unmarried.)

40

PETRUS[3] VIELE, of Philip,[2] Aerhnout Cornelisen[1], b. July 5, 1702, m. Elizabeth Louw Aug. 14, 1731, and d. before 1759. Children:

59 Petrus, b. Mar. 12, 1732, d. 1739.
60 Elizabeth, b. Dec. 8, 1734.

61　Anna, b. Dec. 25, 1736, bap. by Domine Vas, d. 1739.
62　Helena, b. Nov. 5, 1738, d. 1739.
63　Margrietje, b. July 15, 1733, d. 1739.
64　Helena, b. Sep. 26, 1742.
65　Margrietje, b. Aug. 11, 1744.
66　Cornelius, b. Mar. 15, 1752.

In the graveyard at Kingston, N. Y., at the present time (1909) there is a stone with the following inscription: "Hier liegt Begraben Anna Viele, Petrus Viele, Margarieten Viele overleden in het jaar 1739 Augustus 12, 13, 26, Helena Viele Augustus 29; Als zyt waaren wy noor lese: Als wy zynsoon meet gy wese." (Which roughly translated means:—"As you are were we before this, as we, must you be.") Within a fortnight these parents—Peter and Elizabeth—were bereft of four little ones between the ages of one and five years, and the least they could do was to put up a stone elaborate for those days. Later other children—Helena and Margrietje—bear the names of the departed. Peter himself died before his father Philip (1761), who mentions in his will his grandson, Cornelius, son of Peter.

1738. Petrus Viele, Sergeant in Foot Co. of Ulster Co. Militia (Capt. Tjerck de Witt.) (Doc. His. of N. Y., Vol. IV, p. 229).

1740. Peter Viele, freeholder in Dutchess Co. (Doc. His. N. Y.).

Elizabeth, dau. of Cornelis Louw and Margaret his wife. In his will (His. Soc. Wills, Vol. IV, p. 193), dated Feb. 3, 1745, he calls himself, "Cornelius Louw of Newark, New Jersey, Gent.," and mentions his daughter, "Elizabeth, wife of Peter Vielle." He d. 1748.

41

AERHNOUT[3] VIELE, of Philip,[2], Aerhnout Cornelisen[1], b. July 1, 1704, m. Catrina van Keuren. Children:

67　Tjerck, b. Feb. 16, 1735.
68　Johannes, b. Jan. 2, 1737, wit: Johannes Viele and Annetje Viele.

69 Johannes, b. Mar. 13, 1738.
70 Annetjen, b. Nov. 11, 1739, wit: Philippus Viele
     and Antje Louw.
71 Mareitje, b. Nov. 29, 1741.
72 Leidia, b. Jan. 31, 1748.

1740. Arnout Ville, freeholder in Dutchess Co. (Doc.
His. N. Y., Vol. IV, p. 205.)

"In 1742 died Tjerck van Keuren, of Kingston, whose dau.
Catrina married Aerhnout Viele." (Mun. Col., Vol. I.)

1748. Arnout Viele, Justice of the Peace, holding Court
of General Sessions at Poughkeepsie.

1752. When the will of N. Hoffman was proved Aerhnout
Viele is mentioned as Justice of the Peace.

1760. Aerhnout Viele witness to a will, that of Philip
Nuker. (Fernow's Cal. of Wills, p. 299.)

43

CORNELIS[3] VIELE (cordwainer), of Philip,[2] Aerhnout Corneli-
     sen[1],
m. Elizabeth Louw Oct. 10, 1734, d. Jan. 1783. Children:

73 Christina, bap. June 27, 1735, m. Tjerck van Vlit,
     Apr. 18, 1772.
74 Anna, bap. May 22, 1737.
75 Johannes, bap. Dec. 26, 1738.
+76 Annetje, bap. Apr. 19, 1741, m. Petrus van Wag-
     enen Feb. 23, 1781.
+77 Elizabeth, bap. Aug. 28, 1743, m. Abram Vosburg.
78 Petrus, bap. Nov. 3, 1745.
79 Petrus, bap. Feb. 21, 1748, m. Neeltje van Kleeck.
     (His. Soc. Wills, Vol. IX, p. 276.)
80 Cornelis, bap. 1750.
+81 Maria, bap. Mar. 8, 1752, m. Michal Farrell, Jan. 12,
     1783.
+82 Cornelis, bap. July 13, 1755, m. Sara van Vlit Aug.
     21, 1786.

+83   Johannes, bap. July 30, 1758, m. Wyntie Sikkels
        Oct. 4, 1785.
84   Gerrit, bap. Feb. 1, 1761.

Cornelis member of Foot Co. Militia of Cor. of Kingston
(Capt. Tjerck de Witt.) (Doc. His., N. Y., Vol. IV, p. 229).

1770. Warrant of Survey to determine lands of Cornelis
Viele and others in Dutchess Co.

1771. Pet. of Cornelis Viele and others for patents in
Poughkeepsie.

1771. Cornelis Viele witness to will of Jacobus De Le-
mettre July 19. (His. Soc. Wills, Vol. VIII, p. 15.)

1772. The will of Elizabeth van Kleek speaks of daughter
Neeltje, wife of Peter Feeler. (His. Soc., Abt. of Wills.)

1783. Received the will of Cornelis Viele (in Dutch.)
Proved Mar. 29, 1783. (Mun. Col., Vol. II, p. 128.)

44

GERRIT[3] VIELE, of Philip,[2] Aerhnout Cornelisen[1],
  b. Sep. 8, 1711, bap. in the First Ref. Ch., Kingston, m. Catharina Bratt Dec. 24, 1746. (Kingston Ch. Rec.) Children:

85   Andrew, b. Sep. 15, 1749. Never married.
+86   Philip, b. Oct. 4, 1747, m. 1st, Maria Bratt June 11,
        1772, at Schenectady, N. Y.; 2d, Maria Vander-
        burg Jan. 1, 1787.

1711. Gerrit Viele, of New York, stands witness to the
baptism of this Gerrit. "Gerrit Philip lived in Ulster Co. and
was a brass founder and blacksmith and had two sons and
two slaves." (Sheldon Viele.)

1738. Member of Foot Co. of the Cor. of Kingston, Ulster
Co., N. Y. (Capt. Tjerck de Witt.)

1760. Catharina, wife of Gerrit Viele, has a sitting in the
Dutch Ch. at Albany. (Albany Ref. Ch. Rec.).

Andrew Gerrit Viele is recorded as a corporal in the 4th
Company 1st Regiment of the Line, entering the company on
Nov. 8, 1776. (Robert's N. Y. in the Revolution, p. 127.) He
appears to have been a soldier of fortune. His greatnephew,

Sheldon Viele, says speaking from tradition:—"He is said to have been in the American army at West Point at the time of Arnold's treachery, and was lame from a wound received in some engagement. He was of a roving disposition, and father (Daniel Viele) says that when he was here about 1809 he was a sailor. He told his mother (Catharina Bratt) that there was one place he wanted to see—Jerusalem—and after that visit he was never heard of again. But Sheldon goes on with his reminiscences and adds that in 1858 his father (Daniel) met some Vieles at Fort Ewen, Ulster Co., and one of them, an old lady, told him that she had known an Andrew Viele in her youth.

Daniel Viele, in writing to Gen. E. L. Viele in 1874, says that Andrew G. Viele, his uncle, never married.

46

MARIA[2] VIELE, of Philip,[2] Aerhnout Cornelisen[1],
  m. Cornelis Wyneitse Vanderburg Apr. 13, 1751. Children (Vanderburg):

> 87 Annetje b. ——, (wit: Philippus Viele and Antje Louw.)

47

HELENA[3] VIELE, of Philip,[2] of Aerhnout Cornelisen[1],
  bap. Sep. 20, 1724; m. Mattys van Keuren July 10, 1747. Children (van Keuren):

> 88 Cornelis, b. Nov. 3, 1754.
> 89 Anna, b. July 24, 1757.
> 90 Tryntje (Catharina), b. Sep. 28, 1760.
> 91 Johannes, b. Dec. 9, 1764.

Witnesses at the baptisms of these children were:—Cornelis Viele, Elizabeth Viele, Christina Viele and Johannes Viele.

Mathys van Keuren had on Aug. 18, 1646, a grant of 40 morgans of land at Harlem. He became a trader and moved to Ft. Orange and from there to Esopus where he died. He married Margriet Huberts and had a son Mattys Mattysen who married Tyntje, dau. of T. C. de Witt. Their son, Mattys van Keuren, Jr., bap. Apr. 24, 1681, married (Mar. 4, 1704), Tryntje Slegt and had six children, the youngest of which was Mattys, bap. Sep. 20, 1724, who married Helena Viele July 10, 1746. The name became van Keuren in 1716. The Catrina van Keuren who married Helena's brother Johannes, was doubtless his sister.

1771. Mattys van Keuren and Mattys van Keuren, Jr., on list of taxpayers in Dutchess Co.

76

ANNETJE[4] VIELE, of Cornelis[3] Philip,[2] Aerhnout Cornelisen[1],

b. Apr. 19, 1741, m. Petrus van Wagenen Feb. 23, 1781. Children (Van Wagenen):

    92　Marytje, b. June 16, 1782.

"Peter, fourth child of Gerrit van Wagenen (son of Aert van Wagenen & Marytje Louw) married Marytje Freer (dau. of Jan Freer & Rebecca van Wagenen who was the dau. of Jacob van Wagenen & Sara Pels), was born at Wagendal, bap. Sep. 15, 1745, married Feb. 23, 1781, Anna Viele, dau. of Cornelis Viele and Elizabeth Louw."

77

ELIZABETH[4] VIELE, of Cornelis,[3] Philip,[2] Aerhnout Cornelisen[1],

b. Aug. 17, 1743, m. Abraham Vosburg Apr. 11, 1779. Children (Vosburg):

    93　Isaak, b. Jan. 21, 1781.
    94　Elisbet, b. Dec. 25, 1782.

Witnesses to these baptisms were Tjerck van Vlit and Christina Filie. Cornelis Filen & Marytje Filie.

46

MARIA[4] VIELE, of Cornelis,[3] Philip,[2] Aerhnout Cornelisen[1], bap. Mar. 8, 1752, m. Michal Farrell, wid. from Ireland, Jan. 12, 1783. Children (Farrell):

95 William, b. Sep. 1784.

Witnesses for this child's baptism, Abraham Vosburg and Elisbet Filie.

82

CORNELIS[4] VIELE, of Cornelis,[3] Philip,[2] Aerhnout Cornelisen[1], b. July 13, 1755, m. Sara van Vlit Aug. 21, 1786. Children:

96 Cornelis, b. Apr. 15, 1787.
97 Abraham, b. Aug. 12, 1788, wit: Abraham van Vlit.
98 Willem, b. Sep. 30, 1792, wit: Willem de Graff and Christina van Vlit.
99 Christina, b. Feb. 11, 1798, wit: Christina van Vlit.

45

JOHANNES[4] VIELE, of Cornelis,[3] Philip,[2] Aerhnout Cornelisen[1], b. July 30, 1758, m. Wyntie Sikkels 1784, d. Feb. 1840. (Mar. Dutch Ch. N. Y., Vol I, p. 13.) Children:

100 Sara, b. June 28, 1789, m. Abraham van Houghtling Feb. 18, 1809.
101 Elizabet, bap. Sep. 16, 1792, m. Jeremiah van Houghtling.
+102 Tjerck, bap. May 10, 1795, m. Elizabeth Barnet Jan. 25, 1817.

86

PHILIP[4] VIELE, of Gerrit,[3] Philip,[2] Aerhnout Cornelisen[1], b. Oct. 4, 1747; m. 1st, Maria Bratt, dau. of Barent Bratt, of Schenectady, June 11, 1772; 2d, Maria Vanderburg, dau. of

Wynant Volkert and Martha Vanderburg, Jan. 1, 1787, d. 1807. Children of Philip Viele and Maria Bratt:

+103   Barent, b. June 7, 1775, m. 1st, Sara Putnam.
+104   Gerrit, b. 1776, m. Susan Vanderburg; d. 1859.
 105   Philip, b. Dec. 28, 1777 (d. at the age of 17.)
 106   Catharina, b. Apr. 11, 1773, m. Asa Daniels, of
        Greenfield, Jan. 22, 1791, at Schaghtacoke.
        (And three who died in infancy.)

Children of Philip Viele and Maria Vanderburg:

+107   Wynant, b. Apr. 21, bap. July 4, 1788, at Schaghta-
        coke, wit: Wynant Volkert and Martha Vander-
        burg, m. Rebecca Welch, d. Apr. 24, 1857.
 108   Mary, m. Aug. 27, 1790, d. June 24, 1792.
+109   John, b. Mar. 1793, m. Hannah Brown, d. Nov. 12,
        1845.
 110   Alexander, b. Aug. 1795, m. Catharine Van der
        Werken, d. June 5, 1797. (Recorded by Pier-
        son.)
+111   William, b. Mar. 3, 1799, m. 1st, Sara Murphy; 2d,
        Martha Stianey, d. Mar. 3, 1845.
 112   Volkert, b. Feb. 24, 1802. Was drowned Oct. 18,
        1832. Never married.
+113   Daniel, b. June 18, 1804, m. Emily Denio Mar. 3,
        1833, d. Nov. 3, 1880.

Philip at one time went to Canada "in the King's service," but this may have been previous to the Revolution for he appears to have been a soldier in the Revolution. Sheldon Viele, of Ft. Miller, says (and I find his memory reliable): "My grandfather, Philip, was living at Schaghtacoke, Rensselaer Co., at the time of the Revolution, and was at the battle of Saratoga or Bemis Heights, Sep. 19, 1777. I think in the Albany Regiment, although at one time he went to Canada as the friend of the King. He was a blacksmith and was probably the first to settle in the present town of Northumberland which is where the fort but not the village of Ft. Miller stood. In 1789 he was Overseer of Highways there. Before his death he moved to the east side of the village and died there

May 31, 1807, within 50 feet of where I am writing. My father, Daniel, born in 1804, lived here till his death in 1880, and perhaps our staying on the spot so many years has something to do with my knowing so much of the family. Grandfather was over six feet in height and built in proportion, and while very strong he was always very good-natured and well-liked." It is curious to find that Philip Viele came to Schaghtacoke to live. This town had been settled by the descendants of Pieter Cornelisen (Louwis and his children) and by those of Cornelis Cornelisen (children of Debora Viele Kettelhuyn), and now came to it Philip, a descendant of the third brother, Aerhnout Cornelisen. A hundred years after Philip, son of Aerhnout, settled at Kingston, the three branches met again. Philip afterwards settled at Ft. Miller, very near to the descendants of Ludovicus Viele, and it was not until Gen. Viele's chart was made that the two branches knew themselves to be related.

102

TJERCK[6] VIELE, of Johannes,[4] Cornelis,[3] Philip,[2] Aerhnout Cornelisen[1],

bap. May 10, 1794; m. Elizabeth Barnet Jan. 25, 1817, d. Feb. 20, 1855. Children:

114   Catharine, b. ——, m. Abraham Van Winkle.
115   John, b. ——, d. 1832.
116   Hannah Sikkels, b. ——, m. James Gray.
117   Wyntie, b. ——, m. Charles J. Mason.
+118   Sylvester Dennison, b. Sep. 27, 1827, m. Anne Gaskings.
119   Sarah Jane, b.——, m. Edwin Stannard.

103

BARENT[5] VIELE, Philip,[4] Gerrit,[3] Philip,[2] Aerhnout Cornelisen[1],

b. June 7, 1775; m. 1st, Sarah Putnam; 2d, Widow Lake. Children by first wife:

120   Barent, b. ——, m. ——.
+121   Asaph, b.——, m. 1st, Sarah Stone; 2d, Esther ——.

122 Polly, b. Oct. 1781, m. Conrad Hartman, d. Sep. 9,
       1889, aged 92 years.
123 Rhoda, b. ——, m. Ira Randel.
124 Cornelius, b. 1817, m. Mary Hinds, d. Jan. 11, 1847.
125 Sally, b. ——, m. Hiram Stanton.
126 Lydia, b. ——, m. Walter Peabody.
127 Phoebe, b. ——, m. Joel Satterley.
128 Susan, b. ——, m. Jotham Felles.

104

GERRIT[5] VIELE, Philip,[4] Gerrit,[3] Philip,[2] Aerhnout Cornelisen[1],
b. 1776; m. Susan Vanderburg in 1796, when he was 19 and
she 14 years of age, d. 1859. Children:

129 Philip, b. 1799, m. 1st, Fanny Hartwell, b. 1797, d.
       Dec. 6, 1827; 2d, Johanna Robertson, and d. Feb.
       7, 1875, "in his 76th year."
130 Nicholas, b. ——, m. Lydia Hyde.
131 Gerrit, b. ——, m. Rhoda Jakeway.
132 Peter, b. ——, m. 1st, Loretta Cromnell; 2d, Har-
       riet ——.
133 Cornelius, b. 1810, m. 1st, Harriet Vanderburg; 2d,
       Mary Ann Blake, d. Aug. 22, 1878.
134 Barent, b. ——, never married, d. 1859.
135 Ashbel, b. 1813, never married, d. Mar. 3, 1834.
136 Mary, b. 1814, b. Archabild Stanton, d. Apr. 10,
       1868.
137 Francis, b. 1814, m. Betsey Carlton, d. 1874.
+138 Johnson, b. ——, m. Rebecca Robinson, d. Oct.,
       1907.
139 Truman, b. Aug. 22, 1820, m. Mary A. Vanderburg
       for his first wife.

107

WINANT[5] VIELE, Philip,[4] Gerrit,[3] Philip,[2] Aerhnout Cornelisen[1],
b. 1788; m. Rebecca Welch, d. Apr. 24, 1857. Children:

140 Emily, b. 1816, m. Stephan Clark, of Gansevoort,
       N. Y.; d. 1890.

141 Elisha, d. in infancy, Berlin, N. Y.
142 Philip, b. ——, m. twice, Gansevoort, N. Y.
143 George, b. ——, m. Angeline Delanarge, Lake Bluff, Ill.
144 Rebecca, b. ——, m. —— Van Kleek.
145 Mary, b. ——, m. Arnold Keys.
146 Sarah, b. ——, d. young.
147 Seth, b. ——, d. young.
148 Elisha, b. ——.

109

JOHN[5] VIELE, Philip,[4] Gerrit,[3] Philip,[2] Aerhnout Cornelisen[1], m. Hannah Brown. Children:

149 Johnathan, b. 1815, m. Betsy Burlingham, d. Nov. 6, 1876.
150 Lucretia, b. ——, m. John Gage, d. Jan. 1901.
151 Lydia A., b. ——, m. David Wells, d. May, 1898.
152 Sidney, b. ——, m. 1st, Mahala Adams.
153 Alexander, b. ——, m. Maria ——.
154 Mary, b. 1827, m. Charles Barrett, d. June 28, 1856.
155 Eliza, b. ——, m. 1st, Wm. David Hazleton, of Marquito Iowa; 2d, Frank Roades.
156 Charles Edwin, b. ——, m. 1877, Elizabeth Rogers (a wid.), d. 1877.
157 Fidelia, b. ——, m. Joel Black.
158 Caroline, b. ——, m. Elisha Cook, Middletown, Vt.

111

WILLIAM[5] VIELE, Philip,[4] Gerrit,[3] Philip,[2] Aerhnout Cornelisen[1], m. 1st, Sarah Murphy; 2d, Martha Stainey. Children:

159 Seneca, b. Sep. 19, 1824, m. Olivia Bridgman July 23, 1854, d. 1898-99.
160 Sidney, b. —— (drowned while quite young).
161 Daniel, b. Jan. 3, 1828, m. Mary Winne July 23, 1852, d. June 15, 1886.
162 George, b. ——.

8

163 Phœbe, b. ———.
164 Sidney, b. ———, d. at Lucerne, Warren Co. He was
a soldier in the Civil War. He never married.

113

DANIEL[5] VIELE, Philip[4], Gerrit,[3] Philip,[2] Aerhnout Cornelisen[1],
b. June 18, 1804; m. Emily, dau. of Obediah Denio and Emily
Starckweather, Mar. 3, 1833; d. Nov. 3, 1880 (Emily d. Jan.
31, 1897). Children:

165 Abigail, b. Mar. 22, 1834, d. Nov. 25, 1840.
166 Maria Lavilla, b. Aug. 23, 1842, d. Nov. 22, 1843.
167 An infant son born and died on the same day, Feb.
10, 1845.
168 Emma Eliza, b. Mar. 29, 1847, d. Mar. 26, 1850.
169 Daniel Taylor, b. Jan. 16, 1849, d. Jan. 30, 1851.
170 Sheldon A., b. Oct. 7, 1850. (Sheldon A. Viele is
a man of remarkable memory and has taken great
pains to keep family records.)

118

SYLVESTER DENNISON[6] VIELE, Tjerck,[5] Johannes,[4] Cornelis,[3]
Philip,[2] Aerhnout Cornelisen[1],
b. Sep. 27, 1827; m. Anne Gaskings, ———, d. Oct. 4, 1856.
Children:

171 Ada Lavinia, b. Oct. 31, 1854, m. Pressley J. Barr.
172 Charles Gray Viele, b. June 13, 1856, at Forksville,
Ill. He is at present (1909) Mayor of Taylors-
ville, N. C.; m. Annie J. Bruner. (Descendants.)

121

ASAPH[6] VIELE, of Barent,[5] Philip,[4] Gerrit,[3] Philip,[2] Aerhnout
Cornelisen[1],
m. 1st, Sarah Stone; 2d, Esther Sotter. Children:

173 Myron, b. ———, m. Esther Mason.
174 Louisa, b. June, 1825, d. May 9, 1847.
174a Esther, b. ———, m. ——— Newman.

138

JOHNSON[6] VIELE, of Gerrit,[5] Philip,[4] Gerrit,[3] Philip,[2] Aerhnout
　　Cornelisen[1],
　　b. Nov. 5, 1818, at Ft. Miller, N. Y.; m. Rebecca Robinson,
　　(b. Feb. 23, 1824, at Ft. Miller, N. Y.), d. Sep. 20, 1907.
　　Children:

> 175　Eugene, b. Dec. 14, 1844, at Sandy Hill, N. Y.; m.
> 　　　Helen Butler Feb. 22, 1871.
> 176　Josephine, b. Apr. 7, 1846, at Sandy Hill; m. Alonzo
> 　　　Perkins.
> 177　Johanna, b. June 4, 1847; m. Daniel Van Buren.
> 178　Ransom Dwyer, b. May 2, 1855.

II

CORNELIS CORNELISEN VIELE

There is no mention of Cornelis Cornelisen Viele with which his name can with any certainty be connected until the year 1665. On August 31st of that year Albany records show that he stood surety for Cornelis Segerman, bidder and buyer of a young mare. To this voucher he makes his mark "with his own hand set." (This Cornelis Segers or Segerman had a farm called Weelesburg on Castle Island. His daughter, Jannetje, married Jacob Jansen Schermerhorn, and their son, Symon, married Willemje Viele (Aerhnout's daughter.) There may be some other notice of Cornelis Cornelisen Viele earlier than this which has been overlooked, for Pearson gives his record from 1661-1683. There are one or two unimportant illusions on the Albany records which might refer to him, and the fact that Aerhnout was there in 1659 makes it seem likely that the other brothers were also there at that time. On Oct. 23, 1668, Cornelis is recorded as buying a bouwery at Schenectady in which he calls himself "Husbandman dwelling at Schenectady." (Mun. Col., Vol. IV.) This bouwery he purchased in company with Claas Frederickse van Petten. (Claas Fredrickse van Petten married Effie, dau. of Arent Bratt and Catalyntje de Vos, and died in 1728. His daughter Diwer married Cornelis, son of Cornelis Cornelisen Viele.) This bouwery was called number 8 and was on the Groote Flaate. It was purchased from Marten Cornelisen van Yesselsteyn, one of the fourteen original proprietors of Schenectady. Cornelis was a freeholder in Schenectady before the grant of Dongan. On Feb. 3, 1670, there is a deed recorded from Cornelis to Jansen Flodder Gardinier, and the same year an item on the Court Minutes records that Cornelis Cornelisen Viele attaches the wheat of Jansen Flodder. In the same year Cornelis Cornelisen buys, with the consent of Sander Leendertsen Glen and Schout van Marcken, a piece of land at "Scheanhectede on North Side River" between Sander Leendertsen Glen and Benj. Roberts on condition of keeping a ferryboat there. In 1671 Cornelis

Cornelisen settled in Schenectady to the occupation of innkeeper, and remained so engaged until the time of his death. In 1671 he took out a license to sell strong drink in Schenectady. His was at that date the second tavern in the town, and was situated on the south corner of State Street and Mill Lane, near the ancient church. There seems to have been an amusing rivalry between him and the other tapster, Acques or Akus Cornelisen van Slyck. Van Slyck was a half breed Indian and, like the Vieles, an Indian interpreter. He had been until the advent of Viele seemingly the only tapster in Schenectady, and naturally resented his arrival. Indeed, Cornelis seems to have had some trouble to get this license, and to have had to press his claim by referring to services rendered to the Indians. It was at Viele's Tavern that in 1690 the traditional merrymaking was going on when the French and Indians swept down, "like a wolf on the fold," and destroyed the little settlement. Cornelis himself at this time was doubtless dead, for it is recorded (General Entries 83) that he was succeeded here by his niece, Maria Viele. Pearson calls her his granddaughter, but we must believe that Aerhnout's daughter was his niece. Aerhnout himself seems to have taken out a permit to keep an inn, and he may have been here associated with his brother. At any rate his daughter Maria married Douve Aukes, who also assisted in the keeping of the inn and to whom after the death of Cornelis it seems to have belonged. The following is a copy of the above mentioned license: "Lycence for Cornelys Cornelysen Viele of Schenechtidy to taap strong Beer and Liquors etc.: Whereas Cornelys Cornelysen Viele of Schenechtide having made this addresse to yet commissarys att Albany to keep an Ordinary in recompence to severall services done by him between us and ye Moques the which they have recommended to mae for my approbation but in regard that there is a person there already by name Acques Cornelysen Gautsh (van Slyck) an Indian that doeth ye same by licence and appointment of my predecessor, Col. Richard Nicoles, would give no determination thereon. And it being likewise represented that ye said Acques hath not sufficient accomodacon for strangers which ye said Cornelys Cornelysen Viele doth promise to bee well provided of for ye relief of strangers and travellers. Upon consideration had there upon I have thought fitt to grant ye request of ye said Cornelys Cornelysen Vielen and by these presents do give him fre licence and liberty to tap or sell by Retayle strong Beer and Liquors to strangers and Travellers at Schenectide with this proviso that this licence now granted shal not take away ye privilege of the former licence given by my predecessor to Acques. And that ye said Cornelys Cornelysen doe keep fitting accommodacons for men and horses but does not presume to sell any strong Liquors to ye Indians to cause any destruction that way under ye penalty of forfeiting this licence and paying such ffine as ye law may require. Given under my hand etc." Signed by Gov. Lovelace.

On May 6, 1672, a dispute having arisen between the two above-named tapsters, Gov. Lovelace ordered that both have licenses to tap without molesting the other. But in this year or the next there appears a third applicant to sell strong drink in Schenectady, and this no other than Juffrouw van Curler, widow of Arent van Curler, the real founder of Schenectady. She had become in straightened circumstances like others by the devastating inroads of the savages. She made application to Gov. Lovelace for a license in consequence of the loss of her husband in the public service and of her house, barns, etc., by fire. Gov. Lovelace granted her request thinking that the licence would stop the quarrels of the other two tapsters, Cornelys Cornelysen Viele and Acques Cornelys Gautch (van Slyck), the Indian, and "defeat their expectations." (Orders in Council, p. 127, Eng. MSS., XXIII, 149. Col. Doc. II, p. 652.) "She was licenced to sell some rum to the Indians and also some quantity of powder and lead." She continued to reside in Schenectady until her death in 1676.

On the 15th of August, 1671, Cornelis Viele received a patent to confirm to him a parcel of land at Schenectady on the north side of the Mohawk River, "Beginning at a certain oaken tree marked on the east and west sides thereof, and so goes alongst the river S S, east of ye bend, containing in breadth 130 rods, and from ye bend goes again northwest 106 rods, lyeing south (north) west from ye hindmost lot of bouwland belonging to Gerrit Bancker, and running along ye bush or Woodside northwest, its in lenghth 132 rods; together all ye saide land as it lyes, having been markt by ye Indians at the utmost limits thereof; as also a certain island (Sassians) bounded on ye south side by ye Magaaees river over against ye north end of Jacques Cornelissen's (Van Slyck's) Island, on the northeast side with a creek or kil that lies by the aforementioned Moeke of bouwland, containing in bigness 14 acres, or 7 morgens of land." (Patent III, 64. Deed v. 198.)

On July 3, 1672, the first patent for the township of Schenectady is granted and also a deed to the Indians. This deed was interpreted to the Indians by Cornelis Cornelisen Viele in the absence of Jacques (Acques, also Akus) Cornelis. This last must have been the regular interpreter. He was often associated as interpreter with Aernhout Cornelisen Viele, and it is sometimes puzzling in the records to know which of them is meant. In fact, Aernhout is sometimes called "Akus." In 1681 the record states charges against Cornelis Cornelisen Viele "Squashed."

In Court Minutes, 1680-85, Cornelis Viele reports that French trappers coming to Schenectady from the Sinekis country told that war had been declared by Holland and France against England, and that the Governor of Canada has pardoned and called up all the Courreurs des bois, 600 or 700 in number.

Cornelis Cornelisen Viele and Claas van Petten took out a mortgage when they purchased the bouweries No. 8, and the Schenectady records say that in 1670 the mortgage was satisfied as regards Cornelis Viele but not as regards van Petten. (Mun. Col., Vol. IV, p. 449.) Probably this was done when in 1670 he made over his moity of the No. 8 bouweries to Jurriaen Teunise Tappen of Albany, in exchange for a house and lot on the west corner of State and South Pearl Streets, in Albany. This Albany deed dated Aug. 26, 1670, I find recorded as from Jurrian Jansen Tappen and the lot is described as "bounded N. and W. by streets south by Ally to the Kil east land of Aerhnout Cornelisen Viele." On Oct. 21, 1673, the deposition of Cornelis Cornelisen Viele states that he had conveyed his house and lot in Albany to Richard Pretty. (Mun. Col., Vol. III, p. 97.)

Cornelis Viele, Sr., also had a gift of land from the natives at that Aal Plaats on the north side of the river. This tract extended two miles down the river and five miles into the wood. The certificate is dated the 12th of Feb. 1719, and states that

Viele had had possession thereof 18 years, and then had sold it
to his daughter, Jannetje, wife of Johannes Dyckman, who left it
at the time of the massacre, in 1690, after occupying it two years.
The wife of Cornelis Cornelisen Viele, as given by Pierson, was
Suster—Pearson adds, "Possibly of Mohawk blood." The very
friendly relations of the Vieles with the Mohawks, the office of
interpreter which one of them so often, and another occasionally, held, the gifts to two of them of lands from the Indians ex-
pressly stated to be for kindnesses received, all show that famil-
iarity and friendship with the red man which could only come
from close connection with him. Suster means "sister," and
she may have been sister to some Mohawk chief. No Dutch
woman seems to have had a similar cognomen. The last mention of Cornelis Viele, Sr., is in 1686, when he and others pe-
titioned for redress for his niece, daughter of his brother Pieter,
at that time deceased, from the cruelty of her stepfather, van
Hoek. Between that date and 1690 he must have died. Of Suster there is no record beyond mention of her as his wife and the
fact that her name was handed down to some of her descendants.

By McMurray Cornelis Cornelisen is credited with six sons
besides daughters, and Pearson credits him with three sons and
two daughters. Neither of these seems correct. Unsparing pains
have been taken in these pages to place the children of these
brothers where they belong.

CORNELIS CORNELISEN VIELE. First heard of in Beverwyck,
1665, and in Schenectady, N. Y., in 1670, when he takes up
lands there; died before 1690; m. Suster—"possibly of Mohawk blood." (Pearson). Children:

+300　Jannetje, b. ——, m. Johannes Dyckman (b. 1662)
before 1688.

+301　Cornelis, Jr., b. ——, m. Diwar (Debora) van Petten.

+302　Debora, b. ——, m. Daniel Kettlehuyn Aug. 16,
1696.

+303　Peter, b. ——, m. Anna Myndertse Van der Bogert
Mar. 17, 1704.

300

JANNETJE[2] VIELE, of Cornelis Cornelisen[1],

m. Johannes Dyckman (born 1662). The Schenectady records tell us that: "Cornelis Viele Senior also had a gift of land from the natives at the Aal Plaats on the north side of the river. This tract extended two miles down the river and five miles into the woods. The certificate is dated the 12th of February, 1718-9, and states that Viele had possession thereof 18 years and then sold it to his dau. Jannetje, wife of Johannes Dyckman, who left it at the time of the massacre after occupying it two years. Dyckman and his family then went to Dutchess County, but in 1715 removed to the Manor of Livingston where Dyckman enjoyed some prominence. Children (Dyckman):

304 Johannes, b. 1690.
305 Maryke, b. about 1688, m. Laurens Knickerbocker about 1707. (N. Y. Gen. & Biog. Rec., Vol. XXXIX, p. 36.)

Johannes Dyckman, b. 1662, was the son of Johannes Dyckman and Maria Bosyns. Johannes Dyckman, Sr., came out in 1651 and served as "first clerk" & commissary to the West India Co. at Ft. Orange, but in 1665 was laid aside by reason of insanity. (Riker's History of Harlem, p. 545.) He d. in Sep. 1672, and Maria Bosyns in 1676. They had two children, Cornelis, b. 1647, who m. Jannetje, dau. of Dirck Claasen Pottbacker and Wyntie Roeloffs, and became the ancestor of the Bloomingdale branch of the family, and Johannes, b. 1662, who m. Jannetje Viele as above stated. In Notary Papers, Vol. I, p. 556, it is stated that Maria Bosyns bound her son Johannes out to Major Abram Staats. (Gen. & Biog. Rec., Vol. XXXIX, p. 36.)

301

CORNELIS[2] VIELE, JR., Cornelis Cornelisen[1],

m. Diwar (Debora) van Petten. Children:

+306 Suster, b. June 4, 1700, m. Myndert van Gysling.
307 Eva, b. June 11, 1702, m. Peter Eling.

+308   Cornelis, b. Jan. 21, 1705, m. Clara Bosie Nov. 20, 1742, d. 1748.

309   Jannetje, b. Oct. 20, 1707, m. Adriaan van Slyck for his first wife, Oct. 17, 1736, d. before 1741.

+310   Nicholas (Claas) b. Oct. 1710, m. 1st, Catlyntje, dau. of Arent Schermerhorn, May 24, 1736; 2d, Neeltje, dau. of Johannes Schermerhorn, Mar. 2, 1744-5.

311   Margrietje, bap. May 3, 1713, m. Jan Eckerman for his second wife, June 3, 1733.

312   Catrina, bap. Mar. 31, 1716, m. Albert Areutsen Vedder June 3, 1738.

+313   Jan (Johannes), bap. Sep. 24, 1719, m. Debora, dau. of Abraham Glen Apr. 15, 1749.

This was the Cornelis who was the adopted son of Douw Aukes and to whom he conveyed when 80 years of age, all his lands in Schenectady. Some of this was land that had been taken up by Cornelis, Sr., and had somehow come into Aukes' possession. "Benjamin Roberts owned a farm at Maalwyck west of Vieles', also the land opposite on the south side of the river, called Poversens, which he sold to Hend. Lamb. Bout and Bout to Viele, of which said lands were confirmed by patent of date of Sep. 29th, 1677, and by Bout's son to Douw Aukes who conveyed the same to his adopted son, Cornelis Viele, Jr., son of the first Cornelis. (Pearson's History of the Schenectady Patent.) After Robert's death his farm came into possession of his two stepsons, Pieter and Joseph Clement. The former sold his share to Cornelis Viele, Jr., in 1710, being the westerly moity—this was conveyed for the sum of £445 (ditto). In 1720 Cornelis Feele is on the list of freeholders of Schenectady. 1733, Nov. 3, Cornelis Feeling took out Letters of administration of the estate of Doww Aakis who died intestate. (His. Soc. Absts. of Wills, Vol III, p. 126.)

302

DEBORA[2] VIELE, of Cornelis Cornelisen[1],
  m. Daniel Kettlehuyn of Albany Aug. 16, 1696. Children (Kettlehuyn) :

314 Gretchen, b. 1698.
315 Anna, b. 1702.
316 Suster, b. 1704.
317 Joacham, b. 1705.
318 Douv, b. Oct. 5, 1707.
319 Douv, b. Dec. 19, 1708.
320 Cornelis, b. 1711, bap. Mar. 11, in Schenectady.
321 David, b. Oct. 18, 1712.
322 Grietje, b. Apr. 24, 1715.
323 Margrietta, b. Jan. 24, 1722.

"1695, Aug. 16, Daniel Kettlehuyne j. m. living at N. A. and Debora Vile j. d. living at Schenectady."

Daniel Kettlehuyn was one of three brothers, sons of Joacham Kettelhuyn Van Cremyn who settled in Beverwyck in 1642. (Mun. Col., Vol. I, p. 73.) The name is spelt in many ways. It finally became Kittle. 1708-9 Daniel Kettlehuyn took up land in Schaghtacoke together with Louwis Viele, Johannes de Wandalaer, Jr., Johannes Harmensen Knickerbocker and several others.

1720. On the list of the inhabitants of Schaghtacoke is Daniel Ketlyne.

303

PETER[2] VIELE, of Cornelis Cornelisen[1],
m. Anna Myndertse Van der Bogert Mar. 17, 1704. Children:

324 Suster, bap. Apr. 29, 1705. (Pearson.)
+325 Meindert, bap. June 20, 1708; m. 1st, Elizabeth Douv; 2d, Rebecka Palmetier, 1740.
326 Susje, b. 1710.
327 Helena, b. May 25, 1713.
328 Jannetje, b. Feb. 8, 1716. ("Baptized in Pokeepsey.")

1714. Peter Viele on list of inhabitants of Dutchess Co., which states that his family consisted of 1 male bet. 60 and 16, 1 male under 16, 1 female bet. 60 and 16, and two females under 16.

1727. Com. Peter Viele and A. de Graff to supervise the estates of intestates in Dutchess Co.

On the *first* tax list of Dutchess Co., 1717-8, Pieter Vielee taxed for £22.

The first deed in Liber A of Poughkeepsie Deeds is a lot sold for building the church on. One of those to whom it was sold (probably as trustee) was "Peter Fillee yeoman."

Deborah van Petten was the daughter of Claas Frederickse van Petten who, in 1668, took up lands in Schenectady with Cornelis Cornelisen Viele. Pearson has mixed up the marriages of Cornelis Viele, Jr., and Cornelis Arentsen Viele, which, fortunately, the records of N. Y. Marriages clears up. Diwar van Petten is the only recorded wife of Cornelis Viele, Jr.

306

SUSTER[3] VIELE, of Cornelis, Jr.,[2] Cornelis Cornelisen[1],
   m. Myndert van Gysling, d. 1772; will, Apr. 2, 1771, proved Sep. 22, 1772. His. Soc. Wills, Vol. XIII, p. 66.) Children:

329 Elias, b. ——.
330 Cornelis, b. ——.
331 Jacob, b. ——.
332 Peter, b. ——.
333 Catharine, b. ——, m. Samuel Arent Bratt.
334 Debora, b. ——, m. Isaac P. Switts.
335 Jacomintje, b. ——, m. Aaron Schermerhorn.

Myndert, son of Elias V. Gysling, who came from Zeeland with his wife, Tryntie Claase, in 1659, in the "Bonte Koe," and took up lands with Pieter Cornelisen Viele in 1670 in Schenectady.

1720. Mindert Gysling, freeholder in Schenectady. (Doc. His. N. Y., Vol. I, p. 370.)

308

CORNELIS[3] VIELE, of Cornelis, Jr.,[2] Cornelis Cornelisen[1],
   b. Jan. 21, 1705; m. Clara, dau. of Philip Bosie, Nov. 20, 1742.

Cornelis was killed in the so-called massacre at Beukendal in 1748. Children:

336 Debora, b. July 17, 1743, m. Frederick Fredericksen van Petten May 3, 1764.

+337 Philip, b. July 7, 1745, m. Rachel Fonda, dau. of Jacob Fonda, Nov. 24, 1770.

1746. "Two gardens lying next Cornelis Viele's pasture" "As it lies in fence next to Cornelis Viele's pasture." (Will of G. S. Vedder.)

310

NICHOLAS[3] (CLAAS) VIELE, of Cornelis, Jr.,[2] Cornelis Cornelisen[1],

b. Oct. 1710; m. 1st, Catlyntje, dau. of Arent Schermerhorn, May 14, 1736; 2d, Neeltje, dau. of Johannes Schermerhorn, Mar. 2, 1744-45.

He is the Claas after which the island in the Mohawk River near Schenectady (referred to in Pearson's Sch. Pat.) is named.

"The next island above Guise's Island is Sassian's or Claas Viele's island, 7 or 8 morgans (about 15 acres). Sassian sold it to Douv Aukes and he to his adopted son Cornelis Viele. The Vieles long possessed it."

MacMurray says:—"This land long remained in the Viele family, and the ancient house was standing between the two locks within the memory of many people now living." (1884) (Deed v. 189.) In 1771 Claas Viele is living on the upper end of Maalwyck. He made his will Apr. 20, 1795, in which he speaks of wife, Neeltje, and daughters Gezina, Catalyntje, Jannetje and son Cornelis. The will of Johannes Schermerhorn, of Schenectady (Oct. 1752), mentions daughter Neeltje, wife of Claas Viele. (Anjou's Cal. of Wills, p. 345.) Children:

338 Debora, b. Oct. 24, 1736, m. Philip van Petten Mar. 29, 1765.

339 Arent, b. Dec. 7, 1738.

340 Catlyntje, b. 1742.

341 Engeltje (Angelica), b. Jan. 26, 1745.

342 Cornelis, b. Oct. 8, 1749.

343 Engeltje (Angelica), b. Oct. 6, 1751, m. Nicholas van Petten.

344 Catlyntje, b. Apr. 28, 1753 (alive in 1795).

345 Jannetje, b. Dec. 1, 1754.

346 Cornelis, b. Jan. 11, 1756 (alive in 1795).

347 Gezina, b. Mar. 2, 1760, m. Lawrence Schermerhorn. ("Nicholas Viele had a daughter Geesje (Gazina) who married Louwis (Lawrence) Schermerhorn. He died in Rotterdam Mar. 26, 1836, aged 88 years, and she died Sep. 26, 1847, aged 87 years.") 1775, July 21, Geesje Vielen and Lawrence Schermerhorn (N. Y. Marriages, O'Callyhan.)

348 Jannetje, b. May 9, 1762, d. Sep. 26, 1841.

1773. Reference to slave of Claas Viele. (Eng. Mass., p. 818.)

1787. Reference to another slave of his. (Eng. Mass., p. 820.)

313

JOHANNES[3] VIELE, of Cornelis,[2] Cornelis Cornelisen[1],
bap. Sep. 24, 1719; m. Debora, dau. of Abraham Glen, Apr. 15, 1749. Children:

349 Debora, b. Jan. 28, 1750; m. 1st, Abraham J. van Epps; 2d, William Kirkpatrick.

350 Margrieta, b. Apr. 29, 1753, m. Eldert Ament, merchant, 1790. He d. before 1798.

351 Maria, b. Sep. 7, 1755, m. Johannes A. van Antwerpen.

352 Cornelis, b. Dec. 18, 1759, d. in infancy.

353 Susanna, b. Apr. 11, 1760, m. Johannes van V (F)ranken. (First Ch. bap. 1782.)

WILL OF JOHN VELEN OF SCHENECTADY.

In the Name of God. Amen. I, John Velen of Schenectady being weak in body, I leave to my wife all my real and personal estate, so long as she remains my widow, "she making no waste or destruction." After her death I leave all to my four daughters, Deborah, Margaritie, Maria, and Susanna. My executors may sell my negro man "Dick" in case there should be occasion for it, to pay my debts. I make Jacobus Peck, carpenter, and Albert Vedder, carpenter, executors. Dated Aug. 15, 1760. Witness: Hendricus Vedder, Barent Vedder, Caleb Beck, merchant. Proved June 17, 1770. (His Soc. Abt. of Wills.)

325

MYNDERT[3] VIELE, of Peter,[2] Cornelis Cornelisen[1],
m. 1st, 1700, Elizabeth Douw; 2d, Rebecka Palmetier, 1740.
Children:

    354 Volkert, b. 1736. (Wit. Margaret Douw and Vol-
         kert.)
    355 Barent, b. ——.
    356 Pieter, b. ——.
    357 Baltus, b. ——.
    358 Johannes, b. ——.
    359 Rebecca, b. ——.
    360 Helena, b. ——.
    361 Neeltje, b. ——.
    362 Jannetje, b. ——.

1740. Ghetrout Mindert Vilen met Rebecka Palmetier.

A Myndert Viele served in the Revolution from Dutchess County.

On May 1, 1765, Baltus Viele and Catharina Losee (N. Y. Mar., O'Callyhan.)

A Baltus also served in the Revolution.

A Baltus S. Viele, of Dutchess Co., married Jane Vermilye 1785. Will of Myndert Viele proved 1786.

337

PHILIP[4] VIELE, of Cornelis,[3] Cornelis,[2] Cornelis Cornelisen[1],
b. July 7, 1745; m. Rachel Fonda, d. Aug. 7, 1797. Children:

363 Cornelis, b. Jan. 3, 1772 (d. in infancy).
364 Cornelis, b. Mar. 4, 1773, d. in Schenectady Aug.
     17, 1863, aged 90 years, 8 months, 13 days; m.
     Yannecke, dau. of Abraham de Graff, May 27,
     1798.
365 Jacob, b. Oct. 18, 1775.
366 Maria, b. Apr. 19, 1779.
367 Clarissa, b. Oct. 10, 1781.
368 Rebecca, b. Jan. 23, 1784, d. Oct. 22, 1845.
369 Debora, b. Nov. 30, 1786, d. Feb. 13, 1790.
+370 Nicholas, b. July 10, 1790, m. Jane Schermerhorn.
     He d. Nov. 24, 1861.

370

NICHOLAS[4] VIELE, of Philip,[3] Cornelis Jr.,[2] Cornelis Cornelisen[1],
b. July, 1790; m. Jane Schermerhorn, dau. of Bartholomew
Schermerhorn, Dec. 23, 1818, and d. Nov. 24, 1861. Children:

371 Rachel, b. Oct. 4, 1819, d. May 21, ——.
372 Maria Ann, b. Oct. 17, 1821, d. Aug. 26, 1864.
373 Philip, b. Dec. 21, 1823, d. Jan. 13, 1895.
374 Rebecca, b. Dec. 19, 1825, d. Feb. 19, 1852.
375 Catharina, b. Feb. 1, 1828, d. Jan. 8, 1859.
376 Clarissa, b. Apr. 16, 1830.
377 Jane, b. Oct. 24, 1832.
378 Sara Fonda, b. June 19, 1835. Last three living in
     1895.

Sarah Fonda Viele writes to Gen. E. L. Viele in 1895 as
follows: "After considerable research I have obtained the
genealogy of the Vieles residing in Schenectady for six generations. As stated in the accompanying sheet Cornelis Cornelisen was my great-grandfather, and I am descended from him
through his son Cornelis."

The only other item of interest in the letter is that she states:
"My father (Nicholas) said there was a third Viele brother
who settled at some point on the Hudson."

III

PIETER CORNELISEN VIELE

Prof. Pearson says in his History of the Schenectady Patent, "Two brothers of this name (Viele) were among the early settlers of Schenectady, Pieter Cornelisen and Cornelis Cornelisen: Pieter came to Schenectady with his brother Cornelis and in company with Elias van Gyseling purchased de Winter's bouwery in 1670." Pearson continues, "Viele's village lot was confirmed to him by patent of date October 21, 1670, containing as it lies along the highway 200 feet having to the west Bent Bagge and on the east the woodlands: as also another small piece of land for a plantation of two morgans or four acres, bounded west by the fence of Claas van Petten and by the lot aforesaid,—behind on the line of Pieter, the Brasihaen's lot." (Patent, p. 752.)

1672. (May 9) Pieter Cornelisen Viele petitions the Court for a survey of his lot and farm. Granted. (Court Minutes.)

1678. Ludovicus Cobes requests Gov. Andros for a grant of land for his brother-in-law, Pieter Viele.

1684. Lewis Cobes, vendue master, of Schenectady, paid over the proceeds of the sale of Bastiyean de Winter's effects 2,199s. The purchasers were Symon de Backer, Elias van Gyseling and Pieter Viele.

1684. Pieter Viele owned land in Dutchess Co. (Ulster Co. Deeds.)

1684, Dec. 21. Pieter Viele and Jan Janse Younkers obtained a conveyance from the Trustees of Schenectady of the 2nd Flat next above Maalwyck, on the north side of the river, the former taking the easterly 17 morgans and the latter the westerly 16 morgans. (Gen. Entries 33, II, 12.) When Jacomintje Swart, widow of Pieter Cornelisen Viele, removed to Dutchess Co., having married her third husband, Cornelis Vynhout, she conveyed this bouwery on the 2d Flat to her "only surviving son," Louwis, in consideration of which he (Louwis) gave a bond to Cornelis Vynhout and his mother Jacomintje (Jacquamyna there

spelt) on June 2, 1701, to pay all advances made for the settlement of his father's (Pieter Cornelisen Viele's) and his stepfather's (Bennony Arentse's) debts. The deed of Jaquamyna,
wid. of Pieter Cornelisen Viele to Louwis Viele is recorded May
28, 1701 (these last from Index of the Public Records of the City
of Albany from 1630 to 1894, Vol. XIV.) The above mentioned
lands passed away from the Vieles when Louwis Viele being about
to remove to Schaghtacoke in 1708-9, reconveyed them to the
Trustees of Schenectady. (Pearson's First Settlers of Schenectady.)

Jacomintje Swart, wife of Pieter Cornelisen Viele, was the dau.
of Teunis Cornelisen Swart, one of the first settlers of Schenectady. According to her father's will she is the seventh child and
must have been very young when she married Pieter Cornelisen
Viele. After Pieter's death, which must have been in 1685, she
married Bennony Arentse van Hoek. There is the record of the
birth of Gerritje. child of Bennony Arentse in January, 1686, at
whose baptism Jacob Meerse Vrooman, the stepfather of Jacomintje Swart is the witness. Bennony Arentse was killed in the
Schenectady massacre 1690. That he was a hard stepfather is to
be seen from the following document from the Court Minutes of
Albany Co. for 1686: which throws a sad light upon the condition of Pieter's little orphans and shows how primitive was life
on the frontier. "1686, Sep. 17. Bennony Arentsen van Hoek is
called to appear before the Court at Albany on a complaint made
by Cornelis Viele, Jacobus Peck, Claas Laurence, Purmurent,
Johannes Sanders, Esais Swart and Lowrys Cobes, that Bennony
Arentsen doth most crewelly and barbarously beat ye daughter
of Pieter Viele, deceased, of which he is the stepfather which
child being stood before ye justice is found al blak and blew and
ye said Bennony being sent for by a warrant and appearing before
ye Justice doth excuse himself saying she is a whole night and
sometimes half a night out seeking cows. Whereupon ordered
that ye said girl be delivered in ye hands of ye Trustees, Jacob
Merse (Vrooman) and Arnout Cornelisen Viele who are to dispose of her as they shal see meet and if ye said Bennony Arentsen
shal for ye future abuse any of ye children of Pieter Viele upon
complaint they shall be delivered to ye Trustees who shall have

power to dispose of the same accordingly and ye bond of good behaviour given ye tenth day—to remain in force."

After the massacre Jacomintje seems to have fled with some of her children to Dutchess Co. whither some of the Swarts seem also to have gone, and there married Cornelis Vynhout. Her daughter Marytje also married a Vynhout. The last mention of Jacomintje is in 1713, when she and Cornelis Vynhout stand as witnesses at baptism of child of Peter Viele and Anna Myndertse van der Bogert: her first husband's nephew. (Kingston Ch. Rec.).

Teunis Cornelisen Swart, an original proprietor of Schenectady, received alotment 10, on the Groote Flaate comprising 48 acres lying over to westward of the third or Poentie Kil and a village lot east corner State and Church streets. His will is dated July 22, 1677, and is a joint one with his wife Elizabeth van der Linde (or Lendt). He was one of two brothers who came to Schenectady according to Prof. Pearson. He died about 1678, and his wife married 2d, Jacob Merse Vrooman, and 3d, Wouter Ugthof, of Albany. (Ulster Co. Wills, p. 74, and Pearson's First Settlers of Schenectady, pp. 180-184.)

3

PIETER CORNELISEN VIELE first heard of in Schenectady, N. Y., in 1668; m. Jacomintje Swart, dau. of Teunis Cornelisen Swart of Schenectady; d. at Schenectady about 1685. Children:

+400 Teunis, b. ——, m. Elizabeth van Eps, June 16, 1693.
+401 Louwis, b. ——, m. Mary Freer, Oct. 12, 1696.
+402 Marytje, b. ——, m. Arent Vynhout before 1696.
+403 Lysbet, b. ——, m. Marten Jacobsen Delamont Nov. 14, 1702.
+404 Pieternella, b. ——, m. Aert Masten Sep. 9, 1703.

400

TEUNIS[2] VIELE, of Pieter Cornelisen[1],
m. Elizabeth van Eps, dau. of Johannes Durkse van Eps, June 16, 1693. Children:

+405 Jacomintje, b. Apr. 11, 1694, m. Cornelis Pootman.
406 Elizabeth, b. Jan. 8, 1696, m. (probably) Jacob
Korse about 1726. In the Kingston church rec-
ords in 1726 are named as witnesses to a baptism,
"Jacob Korse and Elizabeth Fiele his huys
Vrouw." Page 470.)

"June 16, 1693, Teunis Vile j. m. and Lysbeth van Eps j. d.
both of Schenectady." (Albany Dutch Ref. Ch. Rec.).

Teunis Viele was evidently in Schenectady at the time of
the massacre for there is this mention of him on the relief list:
"Teunis Viele was given 20 ells of cloth as a refugee from
Schenectady."

Teunis probably died before or by 1697, as in this year there
is mention, on the Albany records, of Elizabeth Viele as "the
head of the house." In 1699 Elizabeth married her second
husband.

"July 16, 1699, Jillis van Vorst j. m. living here (Albany)
and Elizabeth van Eps, widow of Teunis Viele, living at
Scenectady; by Johannes Sanderse Glen. Justice." (Albany
Dutch Ref. C. Rec.).

Johannes Durkse van Eps was the grandson of Jan van Eps,
one of the first settlers of Schenectady. He had two wives, 1st,
Maria Damen; 2d, Elizabeth Janse. The last was probably
the mother of Elizabeth.

401

LOUWIS[2] VIELE, of Pieter Cornelisen[1],
m. Mary Frere, dau. of Hugo Frere (Freer), Oct. 12, 1696.
Children:

+407 Jannetje, b. Oct. 26, 1698, wit: Cornelis Swart and
Jacomintje Swart (Kingston bap.), m. Johannes
Ouderkerk May 15, 1720.
+408 Pieter, b. Nov. 3, 1700, m. Catrina van Schaick, June
23, 1728.
+409 Teunis, bap. Sep. 28, 1702, in Schenectady, m. Maria
Fonda Oct. 12, 1724.
+410 Hugus, b. Feb. 25, 1705, m. 1st, Cath. van Woert
Feb. 13, 1728; 2d, Elizabeth van Vechten Sep.
17, 1752.

THE OLD KNICKERBOCKER HOMESTEAD.
SCHAGHTICOKE, N. Y.

WHERE VIELES HAVE LIVED AND DIED AND FROM WHENCE KNICKERBOCKERS
HAVE GONE FORTH TO MARRY VIELES

411 Jacomintje, b. Nov. 9, 1707, m. Isaac Fort for his
first wife, Sep. 7, 1729.

+412 Isaac, b. Apr. 29, 1710, m. Hendrickje Oothout Aug.
5, 1736.

413 Stephenus, b. 1711-2-3.

+414 Abraham, b. Sep. 26, 1715, m. Francintje Fort Jan.
22, 1739.

+415 Jacob, bap. June 21, 1719, wit: Ysak and Mayke
Ouderderk, m. Eva Fort July 4, 1741-2.

"Oct. 12, 1696, Louwis File (Viele) j. m. born in Sknegtede
(Schenectady) and residing and under the jurisdiction of
Kingston and Mary Frere j. d. born in Horle (Hurley) and
residing in Pals (Paltz). Bans published but dates not given."
(Kingston Ch. Rec.).

1699. On Jan. 11, Louwis Viele took the oath at Schenectady.

1708. Being about to remove to Schaghticoke Louwis Viele
conveyed to the Trustees of Schenectady land deeded to him
by his mother, Jacomintje Swart in 1699, when she removed
to Ulster Co. (see acct. of Pieter Cornelisen Viele) 1709. (Oct.)
the City of Albany conveyed the land at Schaghticoke, N. Y.,
to the following persons who settled there at that time:—
Johannes de Wandalaer, Jr., Johannes Harmans Vischer, Cor-
set Vedder, Daniel Kettlehuyn, Johannes Harmensen Knickerbocker, Derick van Vechten, and Louwis Viele.

"Louwis Viele was a man of considerable wealth for those
days, and his Viele's Bridge toll was in operation for more than
a century at Schaghticoke."—(H. K. V.)

1730. Lewis Viele petitions for land at Schaghticoke.

1741. (May 8) Louwis Viele receives £8; a present from
the Council to the Dutch church at Schaghticoke.

1695. Maria Freer stands wit. to child of Hugo Freer, Jr.
and Maria LeRoy his wife.

HUGO FREER (or FRERE), a Huguenot and patentee of New Paltz,
N. Y., was settled in Ulster Co. long before 1700. When the
church was organized at New Paltz (in 1677) it was "with
Louis du Bois as Elder and Hugo Frere as Deacon and having
Pierre Daille as minister." (Olde Ulster.)

Hugo Freer made two wills written in French. In the first one there is the legacy to Maria Freer, of a cow. First will dated 1692, second will 1706-7. Maria is named in both. He married twice. His first wife was Maria Haye, of whom it is recorded "the wife of Hugo Freer died in the Lord." His second wife was Janneke Wilbau. (Kingston Ch. Rec.).

1676 (Aug. 10). Will witnessed by Hugo Freer who makes his mark. (Ulster Co. Wills, Vol. I, p. 31.)

Children of Hugo Freer named in will: "Hugue, Abraham, Isaac, Jacob, Joseph, Jean, and Mary, bap. at Hurley 1676; m. Louis Velle, of Schenectady." (Anjou's Cal. of Wills.)

402

MARYTJE[2] VIELE, of Pieter Cornelisen[1],
m. Arent Fynhout or Vynhout (Jacomintje Swart the wid. of Pieter Viele; m. Cornelis Vynhout for her third husband. Marytje evidently married into the same family.) Children (Vynhout):

416 Neeltje (Cornelia),, b. Feb. 2, 1696; wit. Cornelis Fynhout, Louwis Viele and Lysbet Arentse.
417 Petrus, b. June 2, 1698; wit. Cornelis Swart and Jacomintje Swart.
418 Petrus, b. Apr. 3, 1702; wit. Cornelis Masten and Pieternella Viele.
419 Jacomintje, b. Sep. 3, 1704; wit. Stephenus Viele and Jannetje Elmendorf.
420 Geertie, b. Oct. 12, 1707.
421 Cornelis, b. Nov. 10, 1710.

403

LYSBET[2] VIELE, of Pieter Cornelisen[1],
m. Marten Jacobsen Delamont. "Nov. 14, 1702, Marten Jacobsen Delamont j. m. b. in Col. Rensselaerwyck and Lysbet Viele born in Schenectady, both living here (Albany.)" Children (Delamont):

422 Peter, b. Oct. 1, 1703; wit. Abraham and Cath. Curleyn.

423 Catharine, b. Apr. 20, 1707; wit. Jan Delamont and
Cath. Curler.

424 Catharine, b. 1708; wit. John Bleecker, Jr., and
Maria Schuyler.

425 Peter, b. 1711; wit. Louis Viele and Susanna Wendell.

426 Abram, b. Feb. 10, 1717; wit. Loueys and Maretie
Viele.

404

PIETERNELLA[2] VIELE (Pieternelltjen), of Pieter Cornelisen[1],
m. Aert Masten Sep. 9, 1703 (Kingston Marriages). Referred to as "Pieternella Viele of Schenectady." Children
(Masten):

427 Jacomintje, b. May 7, 1710.

428 Cornelis, b. Feb. 27, 1715; wit. Arent Fynhout and
Lysbet Arentse.

429 Geerjen, b. June 9, 1717.

1703. Pieternella Viele and Stephan Viele witnesses for
child of Adam Swart.

1711. Art Masten and Pieternella Viele witnesses for a
child—Jacomintje.

1714. On the list of freeholders in Dutchess Co. appears
the name of Aert Masten.

On June 14, 1718, Aret or Arent Masten of Dutchess Co.
yeoman, in consideration of £80 bought a tract of land from
Thomas Saunders & Aeltje his wife containing by computation
42 morgans more or less.

1737. Aert Masten member of the Foot Co. of the Cor. of
Kingston, Ulster Co. (Capt. Tjerck de Witt.)

In Anjou's Cal. of Wills, Vol. I, p. 82, is the following entry:
"Cornelis Masten of Kingston (Will dated Jan. 3, 1712, in Willemstadt [Albany]), was the son of John Marston, an Englishman, who settled at Flushing previous to 1644 and married
Dievertje Jans Oct. 27, 1650, and in his will dated 1670 he re-
fers to 'my two sons John and Cornelis under age.' Cornelis
married in 1676 Elizabeth Arentse van Wagenen, dau. of Aert

Jacobsen and Antje Gurje, and had issue, 1st, Johannes; 2d,
Debora, and 3d, Aert, b. Sep. 22, 1682; m. Sep. 1704, Pieternella Viele."

405

JACOMINTJE[3] VIELE, of Teunis,[2] Pieter Cornelisen[1],
   b. Apr. 11, 1694; m. Cornelis Pootman, of Schenectady. Children:

   430 Cornelis, b. Nov. 4, 1713
   431 Teunis, b. Mar. 31, 1716, m. Rebecca van Antwerp.
   432 Elizabeth, b. Dec. 30, 1717, m. Cornelis Groot.
   433 Johannes, b. Mar. 18, 1720.
   434 Lowys, b. Dec. 1, 1722, m. Sara Arents van Ant-
        werp Dec. 6, 1746.
   435 Maritie, b. Mar. 14, 1724, m. Johannes van Vranken.
   436 Catalyntje, b. May 4, 1726 (bap. May 5.)
   437 Jacob, b. July 6, 1729.
   438 Margerietta, b. Jan. 13, bap. Jan. 30, 1732; m. Jacob
        van Franken.
   439 Eva, b. Dec. 16, 1734 (bap. Dec. 22.)
   440 Arent, b. July 31, 1736.
   441 Gysbert, b. June 28, 1741.

Cornelis Pootman was the youngest son of Johannes Pootman (b. 1645) and Cornelia Bratt, his wife (b. 1655), who
were two of the victims of the Schenectady massacre, Feb. 8-9,
1690. They left five small children. Their descendants are in
Schenectady to this day (1909) spelling the name Putman.

1690. "Johannes Potman killed and his wife killed and her
scalp taken off." (Doc. His. of N. Y., Vol. I, p. 305.)

1690. "To Johannes Pootman's children 70 ells of Osenburg linen." (List of Relief Fund.)

Johannes Pootman had been made a Justice of the Peace in
January, 1689-90, by Gov. Leisler. (Doc. His. of N. Y., Vol. II,
p. 149.), apparently just a month before he was killed.

407

JANNETJE[3] VIELE, of Louwis,[2] Peter Cornelisen,[1],
  b. Oct. 26, 1698; m. Johannes Ouderkerk Dec. 15, 1720, for his
first wife. She d. before 1735, for her husband in that year m.
Helena Fonda. He. d. Sep. 1746 (buried Sep. 30.) Children
(Ouderkerk):

> 442 Maria, b. May 31, 1724 (wit. Louys and Maria
>   Viele.)
> 443 Jacomintje, b. Oct. 8, 1726 (wit. Hugo and Jaco-
>   mintje Viele.)

1720. "Dec. 15 (with banns) Johannes Ouderkerk and Jannetje Viele" (Albany Dutch Ref. Ch. Rec.).

1730. Jannetje and Johannes Ouderkerk witnesses at baptism of child of Teunis Viele and Maria Fonda.

1751. Harman Knickerbocker Deacon at Schaghticoke in
place of Joh. Ouderkerk deceased.

1762. Peter Viele having made application to the Corporation of Albany for a parcel of woodland which "this Board will
grant him providing it is no detriment to the farm of the heirs
of Johannes Ouderkerk deceased." (Mun. Col., Vol. I, p.
133.) (Land at Schaghticoke.)

408

PIETER[3] VIELE, of Louwis,[2] Pieter Cornelisen[1],
  b. Nov. 3, 1700; m. Catrina van Schaick June 23, 1728. Children (bap. in Albany):

> +444 Lewis, bap. Jan. 2, 1729, wit: Louys Viele and an-
>   other; m. Sara Storm Nov. 8, 1778.
> +445 Sara, bap. Aug. 2, 1730; m. Isaac Fort for his 2d
>   wife, July 7, 1751.
> 446   Maria, bap. June 4, 1732, m. Louis Hogose Viele
>   Sep. 27, 1756.

Peter Viele settled at Stillwater, N. Y.

1762. "This day sold to Peter Viele a certain parcil of wood
situate, lying and being at Stillwater."

1738. Peter Viele builds a dam.
1742. Peter Viele and Hugus Viele do not pay taxes.
1743. Peter Viele wants more land.

409

TEUNIS[3] VIELE, of Louwis,[2] Pieter Cornelisen[1],
bap. Sep. 28, 1702, in Schenectady; m. Maria Fonda in Albany
Oct. 12, 1724. Maria Fonda (bap. in Albany Jan. 7, 1700) was
the dau. of Johannes Fonda and Marytje Loockermans, m. in
Albany Dec. 5, 1694. (Gen. and Biog. Rec., Vol. XXXIX, p.
186.) Children bap. in Albany:

+447   Lewis, bap. Aug. 30, 1725 (wit. Louwis & Maria
        Viele); m. Annetje Quackenbos (bap. Jan. 15,
        1735, in Albany, N. Y.), 1752.

+448   Johannes, bap. Sep. 17, 1727, m. Geesje Slingerland
        Aug. 15, 1739.

449   Maria, bap. Feb. 1, 1730, m. Hendrick van der
        Werken.

450   Rebecca, bap. Oct. 30, 1732, m. Abraham Slinger-
        land.

451   Stephenus, bap. June 2, 1735, buried Oct. 4, 1736
        (Albany Ref. Ch. Rec.).

452   Stephenus, bap. July 1, 1736, wit: Pieter & Libertse
        Viele (d. before 1737.)

+453   Jannetje, bap. Nov. 20, 1737, m. Joh. Sybr. Quack-
        enbos (bap. in Albany May, 1729) in Albany
        Dec. 9, 1758. Joh. Sybr. Quackenbos was the
        son of Sybrant Quackenbos and Lysbet Knikkel-
        bakker, his wife (bap. Nov. 1, 1702), dau. of
        Johannes Harmensen Knickerbocker and Anna
        Quackenbos, m. at Albany Oct. 19, 1701. (Anna
        was the dau. of Wouter Pietersen Quackenbos of
        Albany, who m. 1st, Neeltje Gysbertse, and 2d,
        at Albany Oct. 4, 1696, Cornelia Bogaert. The
        father of Joh. Harmensen Knickerbocker, Har-
        men Jansen Knickerbocker, the emigrant, m.
        about 1681 Lysbet Janse Bogert, a dau. of Jan

Laurensen Bogert and Cornelia Evertse, b. in
Holland in 1659. (Gen. and Biog. Rec., Vol.
XXXIX, pp. 34-5-6.)

454 Catharina, bap. Sep. 28, 1740.

455 Peter, bap. Oct. 21, 1744, wit: Pieter & Cath. Viele;
d. before 1747.

A child of Teunis, either Peter or Stephenus 2d, was buried
July 8, 1746. (Albany Ref. Ch. Rec.).

1752. "Maria, wife of Teunis Viele has a sitting in the Ref.
Dutch Ch. in Albany."

1755. Teunis Viele's account to be allowed. (Council
Minutes.)

1759. Teunis Viele collects £5 2s. 6d. from the city.

1777. May 6, will of Teunis Viele of Rensselaer Manor:
proved Oct. 21, 1779. In it is mention of wife Maritie and
children: Lewis, Johannes, Maria, Rebecca, Jannetje and Catharina. (Albany Co. Rec. of Wills I. Part II, p. 25.)

410

HUGUS[3] VIELE, of Louwis,[2] Pieter Cornelisen[1],
b. Feb. 25, 1705; m. in Albany, 1st, Catharina Van Woert, Feb.
13, 1728; 2d, Elizabeth Van Vechten Sep. 17, 1752.

456 Louis, bap. Apr. 20, 1729, m. Maria Viele (bap.
June 4, 1732), dau. of Peter Viele, Sep. 27, 1756.
of Ch. in Schaghticoke 1753.

457 Jacob, bap. Aug. 2, 1730, m. Maria ——; members
of Ch. in Schaghtacoke 1753.

458 Maria, bap. May 27, 1733; wit: Joh. & Jannetje
Ouderkerk.

459 Stephenus, bap. Oct. 26, 1735, wit: Joh. & Jannetje
Ouderkerk.

+460 Maria, bap. Mar. 14, 1737, m. Johannes H. Groesbeck July 28. 1755.

+461 Annake, bap. Feb. 17, 1739, wit: Peter & Cath.
Viele; m. Franz Winne, Jr., Dec. 21, 1758.

+462 Sara, bap. Feb. 14, 1742, m. Baltus van Benthuysen
Aug. 5, 1762.

+463 Peter, bap. Jan. 12, 1745-6, m. Elizabeth Fonda (Schaghticoke Ref. Ch. Rec.). Children baptized in Albany or Schaghticoke.)

1749. Elizabeth van Vechten (now Viele) has a sitting in the Ref. Dutch Ch. in Albany. (Munsell's Collections.)

1755. Hugus Viele and Joh. Knickerbocker appear before the Council with regard to rent. (Mun. Col., Vol. I.)

1762. Hugus Viele and Jacob Viele dispute over land. (Mun. Col., Vol. I.)

1766. Deed of land to Hugus Viele of about 40 acres. (Mun. Col. Vol. I, p. 167.)

412

Isaac³ Viele, of Louwis,² Pieter Cornelisen¹,
b. Apr. 29, 1710; m. Hendrickje Oothout Aug. 5, 1736. Children:

464 Maria, bap. July 3, 1737, wit: Louwis and Maria Viele.

465 Lammetje, b. 1740; wit: Aert and Lammetje Oothout.

466 Ludovicus Biblicus Jacobus, bap. Apr. 1, 1743; wit: Peter and Cath. Viele.

"On Aug. 5, 1736, m. G. Viele and H. Oothout." (N. Y. Mar.) The "G" should read "I" (or "Y" as Isaac was sometimes written "Ysac") and Oothout is the name of Isaac's wife whom Pearson simply calls "Hendrickje." The Lammetje Oothout after whom her second daughter is named is very likely her mother.

1742. Isaac Viele, freeholder in Albany. (Mun. An., Vol. II, p. 283.)

1747. Item from will of Stephen Van Rensselaer of the Manor of Rensselaerwyck (June 24), "a lot of ground adjoining to the north of the lot of Isaac Fiele, lying on the west side of the road that leads from the Town to the Manor house being 40 feet in breadth, and as long as the said Fiele's lot." (His. Soc. Abst. of Wills, Vol. IV, p. 144.)

414

ABRAHAM[3] VIELE, of Louwis,[2] Pieter Cornelisen[1],

b. Sep. 26, 1715; m. Francintje Fort "January 2d (with banns) 1738-9, Abraham Viele j. m. and Francyntie Fort j. d." (Albany Ref. Dutch Ch. Rec.). Abraham buried June 28, 1746 (same). Children:

467 Johannes, bap. Jan. 12, 1745, wit: Jacob and Eva Viele.

415

JACOB[3] VIELE, of Louwis,[2] Pieter Cornelisen[1],

bap. June 21, 1719; m. Eva Fort (La Ford.) July 4, 1741-2, d. about 1797 (will of that date.) Children:

+468 Ludovicus, bap. Oct. 17, 1742, in Schenectady; m. Eva Toll Nov. 17, 1766 (see will). Died Dec. 27, 1800.

+469 Abraham, bap. Aug. 25, 1745, m. Annetje Knickerbocker (bap. Mar. 11, 1753, at Albany, N. Y.), Apr. 5, 1771, at Schaghticoke, N. Y., Lic. dated Sep. 10, 1770. (New York State Mar.)

470 Maria, bap. July 12, 1750, m. Jesse Toll (see will).

+471 Stephen, bap. Aug. 3, 1753, m. Sara Toll Sep. 14, 1773. (See will.)

+472 Annetje, b. May 27, 1756, m. Gerrit Winne Sep. 14, 1773; d. before 1797.

+473 Johannes, bap. June 24, 1759, m. Catrina Groesbeck June 26, 1779.

+474 Sara, bap. June 18, 1764, wit: John Knickerbocker and Rebecca Fonda; m. Willem Groesbeck Jan. 24, 1784.

"July 4, 1741-2 (with banns) Jacob Viele j. m. and Eva Fort j. d. (Holland Soc. Year Book 1905.)

1763. Jacob Viele Elder in the Dutch Church at Schaghtacoke, N. Y. (Sch. Ch. Rec.).

1768. (Sep. 12) Jacob Viele witness to will of Herman Knickerbocker. (His. Soc. Abst. of Wills, Vol. VIII, p. 75.)

Jacob Viele and his four sons were Revolutionary soldiers.
Stephen was a Quartermaster—all the rest were enlisted men.
All the brothers were in the 14th Albany Militia, Schaghticoke
and Hoosic districts. (Col. Johannes Knickerbocker.) Jacob
the father was in the 5th Regiment. (The compiler has D.
A. R. Bars for Jacob and Ludovicus.)

Jacob is said to have married a second time, his second wife
being Catrina Coddington; m. in Albany Nov. 10, 1757.

WILL OF JACOB VIELE (1797).

"In the name of God, I, Jacob Viele of the town of Schaghtacoke, County of Rensselaer, considering the uncertainty of
human life and being of sound and perfect mind and memory,
(blessed be God for the same), do make and publish this my
last will and testament in manner and form following: that is
to say—First, I give and bequeath unto my eldest son, Lodevicus, three pounds as his birthright. I give and bequeath unto
Jacob the eldest son of my son Stephen to his heirs and assigns
forever the lot of land or farm whereon my son Stephen now
lives, in the town and county of Saratoga, with this express
condition that the said Jacob shall decently maintain his father
and mother during their life time or if on the death of one of
them, the other shall remarry, he or she shall then be excluded
from any further maintenance from the said Jacob, and further
if it so happen that through disappointment or otherwise, his
father or mother or either of them on the death of one, should
withdraw from the said Jacob elsewhere then the said Jacob
shall pay yearly unto them or on the death of one to the sur-
vivor of them, the sum of twelve pounds during their (his or
her) lifetime or widowhood.

"I also give and bequeath unto all the rest of the children of
my son Stephen my young negro man named Joe, and their heirs
and assigns forever after the death of their father Stephen to
which time it is my will the said negro man shall live with Jacob
and then share and share alike, only Jacob excepted.

"I also give and bequeath unto my son Johannis and to his
heirs and assigns two-thirds of that lot of land in the County
of Saratoga known and distinquished in a map as farm No. 3,

in great lot No. 26 for which said lot of land he shall pay the sum of one hundred pounds lawful money of the State of New York unto my legatees hereafter named in two different payments (that is one half, or fifty pounds in two years after my decease and the other fifty pounds in four years after my decease.)

"To my son Lodevicus the sum of ten pounds in two years after my decease and the farther sum of ten pounds in four years and to his heirs and assigns, and the farther sum of ten pounds after my decease and ten pounds in four years after my decease to my son Abraham and to his heirs and assigns. Also to my daughter Maria and her heirs and assigns the sum of ten pounds in two years and the farther sum of ten pounds in four years after my decease.

"Lastly to the heirs of my daughter Annatie deceased and their assigns the sum of twenty pounds in two years and the further sum of twenty pounds in four years after my decease to be equally divided among them share and share alike.

"I also give and bequeath unto my son Lodevicus and to his heirs and assigns my negro wench, young Bett. I also give and bequeath unto my son Abraham and to his heirs and assigns my negro wench Em. I also give & bequeath unto my daughter Maria and to her heirs and assigns my negro wench Dean with all her children, except her eldest son Tom who I give unto my grandson Jacob Toll and to his heirs and assigns. I also give and bequeath to the heirs and assigns of my daughter Annetie my young negro wench Dean share and share alike—I also give and bequeath unto my daughter Sarah and to her heirs and assigns my negro wench Sue with her children. I also give and bequeath unto my son Johannis and to his heirs and assigns my negro man Tom and negro boy Dick; also three horses out of my stock such as he shall chuse and a plough, harrow, waggon and slay with its tackling, and the remainder of my stock to be divided among all my children share and share alike: and my household furniture I order to be divided among all my children share alike, Except my Linnen such as Sheets and Pillow Cases to be divided among my daughters share alike. I order that my daughter Sarah shall have the remainder of her outset such as my other daughters have had to be given by all my heirs above mentioned in equal proportion which I order my execu-

tors who I shall hereafter name to see it done and I do order all
my close and wearing apparel to be divided among my four
sons share alike and I do order and it is my will that my negro
man Tim and my old negro wench Bet may chuse with which
of my children they wish to live and the one they chuse to live
with shall pay what they may reasonably judge to be worth
and the same shall be paid by him or her to all my children
share alike.

"I do also order that my just debts and funeral charges
shall be paid by all my heirs above mentioned each
their equal proportion and I also order all the debts owing to
me to be collected by my executors and the same to be divided
among all my children share alike, except my daughter Sarah
who is to have no share of my outstanding debts for reason of
her part being already given in the sale of my farm to her husband and—Lastly I do appoint and ordain my two sons Lodevicus and Johannis and Jacob Yates Executors of this my last
Will and Testament. In Witness thereof I have hereunto set
my hand and seal this thirteenth day of July one thousand seven
hundred and ninety-seven.

"JACOB VIELE."

1762. "This Board is of opinion that the land in dispute between Hugo Viele and Jacob Viele belongs to this corporation
and that Hugo Viele and Jacob Viele mow the hay as they used
to do until further orders and that the clerk will acquaint them
therewith." (Mun. Col., Vol. I, p. 132.)

1773. "Recommended by this Board that Jacob Vielen have
leave to cut 100 logs of timber in the corporation right and that
he allow the corporation nine pence a piece, etc. (p. 243)."

Abraham Fort, father of Eva, was the son of Jan Fort or La
Ford of Nistagogone, who died in 1707. (Anjou's Ulster Co.
Wills.) Abraham was a freeholder in Schaghtacoke 1720
(Pearson), and an Elder in the church there 1774-78.) He
married Anna Barber Clute, daughter of Frederick Clute of
Kingston, and Francintje du Mond. Francintje's father, Wal-
randt du Mond, was a prominent Walloon of the early days of
Esopus; an Adelborst in the employ of the East Indian Co. His
will is in Anjou's Cal. of Wills.

444

LEWIS[4] VIELE, of Pieter,[3] Louwis,[2] Pieter Cornelisen[1],
bap. Jan. 2, 1729; m. Sara Storm Nov. 8, 1778. Children:

475 Catrina, bap. Sep. 24, 1779, wit: David Storm & Catrina Viele.

476 Peter, bap. Aug. 30, 1781, wit: Peter Viele and Elizabeth Fonda.

477 Maria, bap. Nov. 4, 1783, wit: Isaac Storm and Maria Fort.

478 Sara, bap. Jan. 5, 1786, wit: Jan Viele & Geesje Slingerland.

479 Hester, b. Oct. 25, bap. Nov. 12, 1788.

480 Daniel, b. Jan. 6, bap. Jan. 25, 1791.

445

SARA[4] VIELE, of Pieter,[3] Louwis,[2] Pieter Cornelisen[1],
bap. Aug. 2, 1730; m. Isaac Fort July 7, 1751, for his 2d wife.
Children (Fort):

481 Daniel, bap. June 2, 1752, wit: Daniel Fort & Gerritse Fort.

482 Peter, bap. Aug. 28, 1753, wit: Peter Viele & C. Van Schaick.

483 Gerrit, bap. Nov. 1763.

484 Jacob, b. May 4, bap. June 8, 1766.

485 Gerritje, b. May 7, 1768.

486 Maria, bap. Sep. 18, 1770, wit: Louis P. Viele and Annetje Viele.

447

LEWIS[4] VIELE, of Teunis,[3] Louwis,[2] Pieter Cornelisen[1],
b. Aug. 30, 1725; m. Annetje Quackenbos (bap. Jan. 15, 1735.)
1752. Children:

+487 Maria, bap. Feb. 24, 1754, wit: Teunis & Maria Viele; m. Benjamin de Witt.

+488 Elizabeth, bap. Jan. 30, 1757, wit: Sybrant and Elizabeth Quackenbos; m. Simon Van Antwerp.

12

489   Teunis, bap. Aug. 5, 1759, wit: Johs. and Catharina Viele j. d.

490   Teunis, bap. Jan. 26, 1762, wit: Teunis and Catharina Viele; m. Cornelia Kip Oct. 31, 1789.

491   Sybrant, bap. Sep. 1, 1764, wit: Johs. Sy. Quackenbos and Jannetje Viele; m. Lena Novelle.

+492   Stephenus, bap. Feb. 3, 1767, wit: Joh. Viele and Geesje Slingerland, m. Jannetje Williams, Oct. 27, 1791.

+493   Johannes, bap. Apr. 3, 1771, wit: Herman Quackenbos and Judith Mabe; m. Elizabeth Woodward Oct. 20, 1793.

494   Catharine, bap. Jan. 31, 1774, wit: Lewis P. Viele and Catharine Viele.

The fact that his younger children were baptized in Schaghticoke and that in 1766 a deed for 22 acres of land in Schaghticoke to Lewis Teunis Viele is recorded seems to make it probable that if he went to Albany he returned to live in Schaghticoke and that he is the Louis Viele who in 1764 is member of the church in Schaghticoke and in 1793 a Deacon there. He was called "Boss" Lewis (a Dutch word) by reason of his forceful, commanding character. There were several Lewis Vieles at the time; all cousins.

Annetje Quackenbos, wife of Lewis Teunis was the dau. of Sybrant Quackenbos and sister of Joh. Sy. Quackenbos who m. Jannetje Viele. She is remembered in the will of her cousin Neeltje Knickerbocker in 1775, "To Annetje, wife of Lewis T. Viele, £15." (His. Soc. Abt. of Wills, Vol. VIII, p. 308.) She also received a legacy from her cousin Herman Knickerbocker in 1778. "I leave to my cousin Hannah, wife of Louis Viley six tablespoons" (the same, p. 75.) Herman and Neeltje were her godparents.

448

JOHANNES[4] VIELE, of Teunis,[3] Louwis,[2] Pieter Cornelisen[1],
   b. Sep. 17, 1727; m. Geesje Slingerland Aug. 15, 1759. Children:

+495 Cornelia, b. Mar. 15, 1761, m. Hendrick Van
     Schoonhoven Jan. 12, 1786.
 496 Teunis, b. Dec. 15, 1762.
 497 Maria, b. Jan. 24, 1764.
+498 Teunis, b. Nov. 19, 1765, m. Barbara Ostrander.
+499 Maria, b. Dec. 1, 1769, m. Peter J. Fort Oct. 1, 1790.
 500 Annetje, bap. Sep. 7, 1771, wit: Ignas Kip & An-
     netje Kip.
 501 Lewis, bap. May 5, 1775, wit: Louis Viele & An-
     netje Quackenbos.
 502 Hester, b. Jan. 4, 1778.

John T. Viele was an enlisted man in the 14th Albany Militia
in the Revolution. (Robert's N. Y. in the Revolution.)

453

JANNETJE[4] VIELE, of Teunis,[3] Louwis,[2] Pieter Cornelisen[1],
b. Nov. 20, 1737; m. Johs. Sy. Quackenbos (bap. in Albany
May, 1729) on Dec. 9, 1758, in Albany. Children (Quackenbos):

    503 Elizabeth, bap. July 1, 1759, wit: Seybrant Quack-
       enbos and Neeltje De Foreest.
    504 Teunis, bap. Oct. 25, 1761, wit: Teunis and Catha-
       rina Viele.
    505 Maria, bap. Oct. 1763, wit: Louis Viele and Annetje
       Quackenbos.
    506 Catharine, bap. Sep. 23, 1765, wit: Ludovic and
       Maria Viele.
    507 Rebecca, bap. Nov. 20, 1767, wit: Abraham and Re-
       becca Slingerland.
    508 Annetje, bap. Nov. 1, 1769, wit: Adriaan and
       Folkje Qwakkenbusch.
    509 Sybrand, bap. Nov. 17, 1771, wit: Wouter and Eliza-
       beth Knickerbocker.
    510 Peter, bap. June 30, 1774, wit: John T. and Geeje
       Viele.
    511 Adriaan, bap. Mar. 1, 1778, wit: Johs. Knicker-
       bocker & Elizabeth Winne. Twin.

512   Lewis bap. Mar. 1, 1778, wit: Lewis Viele & Annetje Quackenbos.   Twin.

"John, son of Sybrant Quackenbos, married Jane Viele and
settled on a farm in Cambridge, a mile below Buskirk's Bridge."

460

MARIA⁴ VIELE, of Hugus,³ Louwis,² Pieter Cornelisen¹,
b. Mar. 14, 1737; m. Johannes H. Groesbeck of Schaghticoke
July 28, 1755.   Children (Groesbeck):

513   Hugo, b. ——.
514   Herman Johannes, bap. Feb. 28, 1765; m. Margarietta Kip (b. Oct. 17, 1772), dau. of Ignas Kip (who
was Elder in the Dutch church in Schaghticoke
1782-88) and his wife Anna Van Vechten.
515   Ludovicus, bap. Oct. 12, 1768, wit: John W. Groesbeck and Maria Viele.
516   Wouter, bap. Oct. 11, 1775, wit: Wouter Groesbeck
and Alida Quackenbos.
517   Pieter, bap. Dec. 13, 1778, wit: Pieter Viele and
Elizabeth Fonda.

461

ANNEKE⁴ VIELE, of Hugus,³ Louwis,² Pieter Cornelisen¹,
b. Feb. 17, 1739; m. Franz Winne, Jr., son of Killian Winne,
Dec. 21, 1758.   Children (Winne):

518   Killian, b. 1759.
519   Catharina, b. ——.
520   Hugo, b. ——.
521   Pieter, b. ——.
522   Rebecca, b. ——.
523   Maria, b. ——.
524   Rachel, b. ——.
525   Jacob Viele, b. ——.
526   Stephen, b. ——.
527   Douv, bap. July 29, 1777, wit: Daniel Winne and
Jannetje Bancker.

462

SARA[4] VIELE, of Hugus,[3] Louwis,[2] Pieter Cornelisen[1],
b. Feb. 14, 1742; m. Baltus van Benthuysen Aug. 5, 1762.
Children (van Benthuysen):

>   528   Hugo, b. ——.

Baltus van Benthuysen, freeholder in Albany 1720 (probably father of above.)

463

PETER[4] VIELE, of Hugus,[3] Louwis,[2] Pieter Cornelisen[1],
b. Jan. 12, 1745-6; m. Elizabeth Fonda.   Children:

>   +529   Catharina, bap. Aug. 1, 1770, wit: Augustin Viele
>   (or Ziele) & Catharina Groesbeck; m. Cornelius
>   Fonda Jan. 8, 1787.
>   530   Alida, bap. July 2, 1773, wit: Isaac and Neeltje de
>   Foreest.
>   531   Maria, bap. June 20, 1779, wit: Joh. Groesbeck
>   & Maria Viele.   Twin.
>   532   Hendrickje, bap. June 20, 1779, wit: Lentie van
>   Antwerp and Hendrickje Fonda.   Twin.

468

LUDOVICUS[4] VIELE, of Jacob,[3] Louwis,[2] Pieter Cornelisen[1],
bap. Oct. 17, 1742; m. Eavau (Eva) Toll (bap. Jan. 15, 1748,
d. May 11, 1835) on Nov. 17, 1766, and d. Dec. 27, 1800.
Buried at Buskirk's Bridge in the town of Hoosic.   Children:

>   +533   Jacob, b. Jan. 6, 1768, m. Catrina Bratt; d. July 20,
>   1826.
>   +534   Simon Toll, b. May 6, 1770, m. Jane Carpenter Jan.
>   6, 1795; d. Aug. 30, 1847.
>   +535   Abraham, b. Jan. 24, 1773 (bap. in Albany); m.
>   Hannah Douglass Apr. 30, 1796, d. May 18, 1840.
>   536   Helsche (Hester), b. Jan. 25, 1775, m. Daniel Car-
>   penter Mar. 19, 1795.
>   537   Eva, b. Dec. 29, 1776, d. in 1779.

+538   Jesse, b. Mar. 22, 1779, m. Sara Fitch.

+539   Stephen, b. Oct. 24, 1782, m. Laura Stearns; d. Oct. 23, 1840.

540   Carel (Charles) b. Nov. 25, 1785. Never married.

+541   Johannes, bap. June 6, 1788, wit: Johannes Viele & Heffie Viele; m. Kathlyne Knickerbocker Nov. 18, 1810, d. Oct. 19, 1832.

542   Ludovicus, b. Sep. 8, 1791, bap. Oct. 30, wit: Gerrit Winne and Annetje Viele.

Ludovicus Viele is said to have gone to Saratoga Co. and there taken up land to the amount of about 400 acres about 1772. The will of Ludovicus is to be found in Fernow's Calendar of Wills, p. 483: it is dated Aug. 16, 1800, and was proved Feb. 18, 1801. In it he calls himself "yeoman of Saratoga" and mentions his wife Eavau and sons Jacob, Stephen, Char (Charles), John, Ludovicus and daughter Hisse. Real and personal estate. Witnesses: Abraham Viele, Jacob S. Viele and John A. Viele.

Still legible on a tombstone in the cemetery of the old village of Tomhannock is the following inscription: "Eva, wife of Ludovicus Viele died May 11th, 1835, in the 88th year of her age." Close by on another stone one reads: "Charles Viele died Sep. 2, 1842, in the 58th year of his age." As he was unmarried perhaps he stayed with his mother all her life; he alone of her large family rests near her.

Eva Toll was the daughter of Simon Toll and Hester de Graff his wife. Simon was the son of Carel Hansen Toll, one of the original proprietors of Schenectady (1661). He came from Norway and married Elizabeth Ruickout, daughter of Daniel Ruickout of Albany. Hester was the daughter of Jesse de Graff, who was freeholder in Schenectady in 1720. (Doc. His. of N. Y., Vol I, p. 371.)

As the Tolls intermarried so much with the Vieles perhaps it will be of interest to insert here the will of Simon Toll.

WILL OF SIMON TOLL.

"In the name of God, Amen, I, Simon Toll, of Schenectady, in Albany County, Mar. 7, 1776. I leave to my eldest son,

Charles H. Toll, my large Dutch Bible and twenty shillings, New York money, for his birthright, wherewith he is to be fully satisfied as heir at law. I leave to my sons, John and Daniel, the lowermost half of my lot of land in the County of Albany, on the north side of the Scatecook creek, at a place called Maghquamekack, with one-half of the saw mill, and privileges of the creek and privilege of the land to lay boards and logs, and they are to make good the value of one-half the saw mill to my son Jesse. I also leave to my sons John and Daniel, all my real and personal estate in the bounds of Schenectady, except as herein given. I leave to my son Jesse the uppermost half of my lot of woodland in Albany County, on the north side of the Scatecook creek, at a place called Maghquamekack, whereon he now lives, with all the buildings, except one-half of the saw mill and one half of the advantage of the creek. I also leave him a negro, Sam. I leave to my daughter Elizabeth, wife of John Farley, a negro girl, Dean, who now lives with her, and a negro boy, Kof. I leave to my daughter Alle, wife of John Mabie, a negro girl. I leave to my daughter Anneca, wife of William Kittlehum, my old negro wench Gen and a negro girl. To my daughter Effie, wife of Lodewikes Fielen, a negro wench Phillis. To my daughter Sara, wife of Stephanus Vielen, a negro wench. I leave to my five daughters, Elizabeth, Alle, Anneca, Effie, and Sarah, all my household furniture and implements, and my wife's bodily apparell, and all horned cattle. I leave to my four daughters, Alle, Aneca, Effie, and Sarah, £300 between them. It is further my express will and order that my dear beloved wife, Hester, shall stay in full possession of all my estate so long as she remains my widow, she making no waste. And if any of my children shall be troublesome, and try to alter any part of my will, they shall be debarred from any share. I leave to my daughter Elizabeth, wife of John Farley, the £60 which I have given her some time ago to buy a lot of land of Frederick Van Petten.

"I make my wife Hester and my sons John and Daniel executors." (His. Soc. Abt. of Wills, Vols. IX, p. 272.)

469

ABRAHAM[4] VIELE, of Jacob,[3] Louwis,[2] Pieter Cornelisen[1],
bap. Aug. 25, 1745; m. Ann Knickerbocker (bap. Mar. 11,
1753) at Schaghticoke Apr. 5, 1771. Licensed Sep. 21, 1770.
(N. Y. Mar.) Ann was the dau. of Col. Johannes Knickerbocker and Rebecca Fonda his wife. Johannes Knickerbocker
was Colonel of the 14th Albany Militia during the Revolution,
and was at various times Deacon and Elder of the church at
Schaghticoke, N. Y. Rebecca was the dau. of Col. Nicholas
Fonda and Anna Marselis. (Nicholas [Claas] Fonda, who
m. Nov. 16, 1716, at Albany, Anna Marselis [bap. there
June 30, 1689] dau. of Gysbert Marselis and Barbar Claaz
Groesbeck, was the son of Douwe Jelisen Fonda and his wife
Rebecca, both in 1683, church members at Albany.) Abraham
d. Aug. 18, 1829. Children:

+543   Johannes, bap. Mar. 20, 1774, wit: Lewis Viele and
Alida Let; m. Margaret Bradshaw (b. Apr. 12,
1771, d. July 13, 1819.)

544   Eva, bap. June 27, 1779, wit: Jacob Viele and Eva
Fort; m. William Winne Knickerbocker for his
2d wife. His 1st wife was Derkje Van Vechten.
He was the son of Johannes Knickerbocker, Jr.,
and Elizabeth Winne his wife. Elizabeth was
the dau. of William Winne, son of Daniel, whose
father, Pieter Winne, came from Ghent in Flanders. William W. Knickerbocker d. 1846.

470

MARIA[4] VIELE, of Jacob,[3] Louwis,[2] Pieter Cornelisen[1],
bap. July 12, 1750; m. Jesse Toll. Children (Toll):

545   Simon, bap. Aug. 29, 1770, wit: Carel Toll &
Marytje Viele, d. before 1797.

546   Jacob, bap. Nov. 2, 1773, wit: Jacob Viele and Eva
Fort.

547   Johannes, b. Aug. 15, 1775.

548 Eva, bap. Apr. 1, 1780, wit: Jacob Viele and Eva
Fort..
549 Helsche, b. Aug. 7, 1782.

471

STEPHEN[4] VIELE, of Jacob,[3] Louwis,[2] Pieter Cornelisen[1],
bap. Aug. 3, 1753; m. Sara Toll (bap. July 25, 1756) Sep. 14,
1773. (N. Y. Mar.) Children:

+550 Jacob, b. Jan. 30, 1774.
551 William Toll, b. Sep. 16, 1775.
552 Eva, bap. July 3, 1779, wit: Jacob Viele and Eva
Fort.
+553 Ludovicus, b. Mar. 30, 1783, m. Hannah Pruyn.
+554 Carel Hansen, b. June 4, bap. Oct. 19, 1788.
555 Hester, b. June 23, 1789.
+556 Simon Toll, b. ——, m. Zernah Hill.

"Stephen of Saratoga" was a Quartermaster in the 14th Albany Militia, Hoosic and Schaghticoke Districts, in the Revolution.

472

ANNETJE[4] VIELE, of Jacob,[3] Louwis,[2] Pieter Cornelisen[1],
b. May 27, 1756; m. Gerrit Winne Sep. 14, 1773. Children
(Winne):

557 Angonetta, bap. Aug. 13, 1774, wit: Jacob Viele and
Eva Fort.

558 Jacob, bap. Jan. 31, 1777, wit: Jacob Viele and Eva
Fort.

559 Frans, bap. Oct. 14, 1779, wit: Adam Vrooman and
Jannetje Ziele.

560 Eva, bap. Jan. 2, 1781, wit: Jacob Viele and Eva
Fort.

561 Frans, bap. May 31, 1783, wit: Johannes Winne and
Sarah Viele.

562   Marytje, bap. Feb. 5, 1786, wit: Jesse and Maria
   Viele.
563   Ludovicus, b. Apr. 9, bap. Apr. 25, 1791, wit: Ludovicus Viele and Avie Toll.

473

JOHANNES⁴ VIELE, of Jacob,³ Louwis,² Pieter Cornelisen¹,
 bap. June 24, 1759; m. Catrina Groesbeck June 26, 1779.
Children:

+564   Jacob, bap. Aug. 23, 1781, wit: Jacob Viele & Eva
   Fort; m. —— Masten.
+565   Maria, bap. Apr. 13, 1783, wit: Johannes Groesbeck
   and Maria Viele; m. Hugh Groesbeck.
+566   John, b. July 3, bap. July 6, 1786, wit: Johs. Groesbeck and Maria Viele; m. Kathalina Pattison
   Nov. 14, 1827; d. Oct. 12, 1859.
 567   Abraham, b. Nov. 13, 1788.
+568   Nicholas, b. June 28, bap. July 10, 1791, m. Sally
   Rogers.

In the history of Saratoga County it is stated that about 1791
Johannes, of Schaghticoke, his brother Stephen, and brother-
in-law, Jesse Toll, took up a large tract of land and settled in
Saratoga County at a place known as Old Saratoga, not far
from Saratoga Springs.

474

SARA⁴ VIELE, of Jacob,³ Louwis,² Pieter Cornelisen¹,
 bap. June 18, 1764; m. Willem Groesbeck Jan. 24, 1784. Children (Groesbeck):

569   Johannes, b. Oct. 18, 1784.
570   Eva, b. July 21, bap. July 24, 1789, wit: Jacob Viele
   and Annetje Viele.
571   Jacob, b. May 7, bap. May 15, 1791, wit: Jacob Viele
   and Marytje Groesbeck.
572   Maria, b. Sep. 4, bap. Sep. 28, 1794.
573   Gerrit, bap. 1800, wit: Gerrit Groesbeck.

487

MARIA[5] VIELE, of Lewis,[4] Teunis,[3] Louwis,[2] Pieter Cornelisen[1], b. Feb. 24, 1754; m. Benjamin de Witt. Children (de Witt):

574 Annetje, bap. Mar. 8, 1771, wit: Teunis and Elizabeth Viele.

575 Johannes, bap. July 23, 1774, wit: Johannes de Witt and Elizabeth Fort.

576 Lewis, bap. Oct. 5, 1778, wit: Lewis Viele and Annetje Quackenbos.

577 Cornelius, b. Sep. 4, 1782.

578 Arriaantje, b. Sep. 19, bap. Oct. 1, 1786, wit: Ignas and Sara Kip.

579 Sybrant Viele, bap. Aug. 9, 1788, wit: Sybrant Viele and Lena Novel.

580 Arriaantje, b. Oct. 3, bap. Oct. 10, 1790, wit: Pieter Fort and Maria Viele.

488

ELIZABETH[5] VIELE, of Lewis[4] Teunis,[3] Louwis,[2] Pieter Cornelisen[1],

bap. Jan. 30, 1757; m. Simon van Antwerp. Children (van Antwerp):

581 Jacobus, bap. Jan. 12, 1784, wit: Douv van Antwerp and Maria Vanderburg.

582 Catharina, bap. Oct. 16, 1785, wit: Benjamin de Witt and Maria Viele.

583 Teunis, b. Mar. 5, bap. Apr. 1, 1787, wit: Teunis Viele.

584 Hendrickje, b. Mar. 5, bap. Apr. 17, 1788, wit: Daniel and Sara van Antwerp.

585 Hendrickje, b. Sep. 12, bap. Oct. 6, 1791.

586 Maria, b. Oct. 30, bap. Nov. 23, 1794.

492

STEPHENUS[5] VIELE, of Lewis,[4] Teunis,[3] Louwis,[2] Pieter Cornelisen[1], bap. Feb. 3, 1767; m. Jannetje Williams Oct. 27, 1791.   Children:

587   Louis, b. Mar. 23, 1792.

493

JOHANNES[5] VIELE, of Lewis,[4] Teunis,[3] Louwis,[2] Pieter Cornelisen[1],

bap. Apr. 3, 1771; m. Elizabeth (Betsy) Woodward, of Connecticut Oct. 20, 1793.   Children:

+588   Anna, b. Oct. 12, 1794, m. David De Garmo.
589   Margaret, b. Mar. 27, 1796.
590   Teunis, b. Apr. 12, bap. May 8, 1798.
591   Elizabeth, b. Mar. 3, bap. Apr. 3, 1800.

1782.   "John Vielen claims the land formerly owned by Adriaan Quackenbos." (Mun. Col., Vol. I, p. 315.)   His mother was a Quackenbos.

495

CORNELIA[5] VIELE, of Johannes,[4] Jacob,[3] Louwis,[2] Pieter Cornelisen[1],

b. Mar. 15, 1761; m. Hendrick van Schoonhoven Jan. 12, 1786. Children (van Schoonhoven):

592   Dirk Bratt, b. July 22, 1786.
593   Geesje, bap. 1788, wit: John Viele and Geesje Slingerland.
594   Cathlyntje, b. Oct. 8, bap. Oct. 31, 1790, wit: Jacob van Schoonhoven and Marytje Spoor.
595   John, b. Oct. 7, bap. Oct. 28, 1792.
596   Jacobus, b. Sep. 14, 1794.

498

TEUNIS[5] VIELE, of Johannes,[4] Teunis,[3] Louwis,[2] Pieter Cornelisen[1],

b. Nov. 19, 1765; m. Barbara Ostrander.   Children:

597   Jacob, b. Feb. 13, bap. Feb. 28, 1796, wit: Jacob Ostrander.

499

MARIA[6] VIELE, of Johannes,[4] Teunis,[3] Louwis,[2] Pieter Cornelisen[1],

b. Dec. 1, 1769; m. Peter J. Fort Oct. 1, 1790. Children
(Fort):

> 598 Elizabeth, b. Oct. 8, bap. Nov. 6, 1791, wit: Daniel
> Fort.
> 599 Teunis, b. Nov. 10, bap. Nov. 10, 1795, wit: Teunis
> Viele and Bethsy Viele.
> 600 Maria, b. Jan. 26, bap. May, 1801.

Peter J. Fort and Maria Viele joined the church (Dutch) at
Schaghticoke May 21, 1795.

529

CATHARINA[6] VIELE, of Peter,[4] Hugus,[3] Louwis,[2] Pieter Cornelisen[1],

bap. Aug. 1, 1770; m. Cornelius Fonda July 8, 1787. Children
(Fonda):

> 601 Elizabeth, b. Sep. 8, bap. Oct. 12, 1788, wit: Peter
> Viele and Elizabeth Fonda.

533

JACOB[6] VIELE, of Ludovicus,[4] Jacob,[3] Louwis,[2] Pieter Cornelisen[1],
b. Jan. 6, 1768; m. Catrina Bratt, and d. July 20, 1826. Children:

> 602 John Bratt, bap. Dec. 24, 1791 wit: Joh. and Marga-
> rietta Bratt.
> 603 Evelina, b. Aug. 8, 1798; m. May 27, 1823, at the
> Viele homestead, Hoosic, N. Y., Rev. Abraham
> J. Switz, son of Gen. Jacob Switz, and pastor of
> the Dutch Ref. Ch. at Schaghticoke 1823-29, d.
> Apr. 11, 1843.
> 604 John Jay; never married. He lived in the town of
> Hoosic, N. Y., and held the military offices of
> Colonel and Brigadier General. He was Assem-

blyman in 1836. "The house in which he lived
is still standing and in good condition." (Letter
from Edwin Buckman of Valley Falls, N. Y., to
Gen. E. L. Viele in 1899.) General Jay Viele
was a man of considerable means, but is said to
have wasted money building bridges over the
Hoosic, which is a treacherous stream, and carried his bridges away as fast as he could make
them. He lived also in Troy, N. Y., and was a
man of courteous manners and pleasing address.

605 Margaret Ann, b. ——.
606 Catharina, b. ——, m. Alexander Marselis Vedder
of Schenectady, N. Y. Dr. Vedder was a practising physician in Schenectady, professor in
Union College and at one time Mayor of Schenectady, where he died in 1878.

534

Simon[5] Toll, of Ludovicus,[4] Jacob,[3] Louwis,[2] Pieter Cornelisen[1],
b. May 6, 1770; m. Jane (Jennie) Carpenter Jan. 6, 1795, d.
Aug. 30, 1847. Jane, b. Sep. 19, 1772, d. Nov. 19, 1844. Children:

+607 Ludovicus Simon, bap. Jan. 25, 1796, wit: Ludovicus and Hester Viele; m. Laville Stearns Jan. 5,
1820, d. Nov. 26, 1882.
+608 Platt Carpenter, b. Aug. 16, 1797, m. Phœbe Bryan
Nov. 15, 1820; d. Nov. 3, 1879.
609 Hester, b. June 12, 1800, d. June 30, 1803.
+610 John Carpenter, b. Apr. 20, 1806, m. Eliza Baker
Oct. 31, 1832, d. Apr. 25, 1880.
+611 Hiram, b. Sep. 5, 1813, m. Abby McFarland Oct. 17,
1838, d. July 25, 1874.

"Simon Viele left Valley Falls early in life and settled in
Fort Miller, sometime between 1813 and 1820, where he took
up a large tract of land, about 300 to 400 acres, the nucleus of
which has continued in the family ever since, and is now occupied by my aunt, Mrs. J. H. Viele." H. C. S.

· 535

ABRAHAM[5] VIELE, of Ludovicus,[4] Jacob,[3] Louwis,[2] Pieter Cornelisen[1],

b. Jan. 24, 1773; m. Hannah Douglass Apr. 30, 1796, d. May 18, 1840, in Iowa. Hannah d. Mar. 16, 1846. Children:

> 612   Philip, b. Sep. 13, 1799, at Schaghticoke, N. Y., m. Catharine Gertrude Brinckerhoff June 4, 1828, d. Mar., 1881, at Ft. Madison, Iowa.

He entered Union College Sep., 1817. In 1821 he began the study of the law at Waterford, N. Y. (possibly with his uncle John L. Viele, who lived there), finished it in Troy, N. Y., and was admitted to the bar Oct., 1824. In 1836 he was Surrogate of Rc. sselaer Co., N. Y. (Fernow's Cal. of Wills, p. 439.) In 1837 he emigrated to Ft. Madison, Iowa, where he lived 34 years. During this time he was four times president of the village and Mayor of the city when Ft. Madison became such; he was three times Judge of Probate for Lee Co., Iowa, and at one time member of the Board of Education in Ft. Madison. He was a man of eloquent speech, courteous manners and had a great love for children. Childless himself his heart went out to all children and at Christmas time he was wont to invite all the children of Ft. Madison to his house and to give them presents. At his funeral two hundred children marched in line to his grave into which they threw flowers.

> +613   Ludovicus, b. 1802, m. Caroline Eliza Hunt (d. Dec. 27, 1865) of Johnsonville, N. Y. (sister of Judge Harmen P. Hunt), d. Apr. 4, 1840.
>
> 614   Patience, b. 1804, m. Daniel T. Newcomb; d. Dec. 22, 1870. She d. Aug. 26, 1891.
>
> 615   Eva Eliza, b. 1806, d. Nov. 12, 1847.
>
> +616   William Douglass, b. 1808, m. Sara M, Newcomb, d. July 19, 1866.
>
> *+617   Delia Maria, b. 1810, m. David Rorer.
>
> 618   Harriet, b. 1812, m. Dr. George W. Fitch, d. Aug. 29, 1847.
>
> 619   Samuel Douglass, b. 1813, m. Margaret Jackson, d. Apr. 5, 1867.

* See pages 124a and 124b

+620   Charles, b. Nov. 22, 1818, at Valley Falls, N. Y., in
       the Viele Homestead, m. Mary J. Hopkins, dau.
       of Judge Edward Hopkins, Dec. 28, 1843, and
       d. Sep. 23, 1901.

Hon. Abraham L. Viele was an Assemblyman from Rensselaer Co., N. Y., in 1812 (Jan. 28 to Mar. 27, and May 31 to
June 19.)

538

JESSE[5] VIELE, of Ludovicus,[4] Jacob,[3] Louwis,[2] Pieter Cornelisen[1],
b. Mar. 22, 1779; m. Sara Fitch. Children:

621   Eva, bap. Nov. 1, 1800, wit: Eva Viele; m. Spiker-
      man? ("One of Jesse Viele's daughters lives near
      him (Cornelius, son of Charles at Red Creek,
      N. Y.). I think her husband's name is Spicker-
      man. She is a woman of remarkable memory."
      Letter of Jacob Viele to his cousin, Gen. E. L.
      Viele, May 7, 1874.) Jesse Viele is said to have
      gone to live in Wayne Co, N. Y.

539

STEPHEN[5] VIELE, of Ludovicus,[4] Jacob,[3] Louwis,[2] Pieter Cornelisen[1],
b. Oct. 24, 1782; m. Laura Stearns, d. Oct. 23, 1840. Children:

622   Jane, b. Mar. 23, 1816, m. George A. Sturtevant, d.
      Mar. 22, 1900.
623   Harriet, b. May 8, 1819, m. Sidney Sutphen, d. June
      3, 1880.
624   Laura, b. ——, m. A. Holland.
625   Lucy Ann, b. June 24, 1824, m. John Allen Thomp-
      son of Pine Plains, Dutchess Co., N. Y., May 9,
      1855.
626   Stephen, b. 1830, m. Martha Ann Shuler Nov. 24,
      1857, d. Feb. 9, 1907.
627   Caroline, b. 1827, m. William Ostrom, d. 1903.

Stephen L. Viele came to Ft. Miller from Valley Falls soon
after the close of the War of 1812. Those who knew

Charles Viele

him spoke of him as a bright man. In 1814 when the
call came to go to Plattsburg to meet the British invaders
Stephen was the Captain of a Militia Co. from Rensselaer Co.,
and becoming out of patience with the dilatory movements of
the rest of the Regiment he started with his men for Plattsburg,
but at Glenville, Washington Co., he met the good news that
victory was ours and he was not needed.   In Ft. Miller he had
a large country store and a commission business.   He was
joined later by his two nephews, Ludovic and John C. Viele.
He was a leading man in the County in his day and respected
for his ability and judgment.   His daughters, who inherited
their father's keen mind, were unusually well-educated for those
days, having attended the Emma Willard School at Troy, N.
Y. (From notes of S. A. V. and H. C. S.). 1836 Hon.
Stephen L. Viele Assemblyman for Rensselaer Co.

541

JOHN LUDOVICUS[5] VIELE, of Ludovicus,[4] Jacob,[3] Louwis,[2] Pieter
     Cornelisen[1],
bap. June 6, 1788, wit: Johannes Viele and Heffie Viele; m.
Kathlyne Knickerbocker of Schaghticoke, Nov. 18, 1810. He
d. Oct. 19, 1832. Kathlyne Knickerbocker was b. Aug. 23
(bap. Aug. 26), 1792, and d. Sep. 16, 1837, "at two o'clock in
the morning." Children:

+628 Louisa Caroline, b. June 18, 1812, m. Dr. Charles
        Winne Sep. 30, 1836.
+629 Rufus King, b. Dec. 3, 1813, m. Phebe Ann Greg-
        ory, d. Dec. 22, 1891.
+630 Augustus, b. Sep. 5, 1815, m. Mary Kenyon, of
        Herkimer, N. Y., Oct. 8, 1839, d. Feb. 12, 1882.
 631 Maria Eve, b. Apr. 2, 1817, m. Johnathan Eustace
        Whipple, and d. Dec. 4, 1842.
+632 Henry Knickerbocker, b. Apr. 29, 1819, m. Letitia
        Thompson, Aug. 5, 1843, d. Aug. 8, 1881.
 633 Sarah Cathalina, b. Mar. 23, 1821. Never married,
        d. 1905.
 634 Maurice Edward, b. July 17, 1823, m. Maria Town-
        send, Apr. 18, 1850, d. 1903, in Albany, N. Y.

+635   Egbert Ludovicus, b. June 17, 1825, m. 1st, Teresa
          Griffin, June 3, 1850; 2d, Juliette Dana, 1872, d.
          Apr. 22, 1902, in New York City.

All the children were baptized by the Rev. Mr. Ostrander
except the last two, who were baptized by the Rev. Mr. Wright.

The Hon. John L. Viele, sixth son of Ludovicus and Eva
Viele, was born June 6, 1788 at Pittstown, N. Y. He received
his education at Union College graduating in 1808. In 1814
he was practising as an attorney at law in Albany. He held
the position of counsel for the Court of Chancery. Report has
it that he served in the War of 1812. He was a New York
State Senator from 1826-29, Judge of the Court of Errors,
au. l Regent of the University of New York. He married
Kathlyne Knickerbocker Nov. 18, 1810. John L. Viele was a
man of mind and energy; he was an intimate friend of De
Witt Clinton and Rufus King. He was cut off in his prime at
the age of 44. He left an honorable name to his children and
children's children.

Kathlyne Knickerbocker was the daughter of John Knickerbocker, Jr., so-called to distinguish him from his father, Col.
John Knickerbocker. The Colonel, a man of over fifty, fought
at the time of the War for Independence as Colonel of the
14th Albany Militia, and Kathlyne's father, a young man of
25, married and already the father of several children, shoul-
dered a musket and served as a private in his father's regiment. There was no standing around for favors in those
earnest days. John Knickerbocker lived to be the father of
fourteen children of whom Kathlyne was the thirteenth. Her
parents lived together 55 years, and when Elizabeth Winne
died on Nov. 10, 1825, nearly seventy-five years old, she left
her husband to linger a year after her. He died on the first
anniversary of her death "at four o'clock in the morning."
Eleven children survived them. Theirs seems to have been
the virtuous and useful lives that give stability to the communi-
ties in which they are spent and pass on as a heritage of bless-
ing to their descendants.

My father (Gen. E. L. Viele) always spoke very lovingly
of his mother, and often mentioned that "Tiny" was her pet

Kathlyne Knickerbocker

name. It has come to me lately that they were calling her "Trintje"—her name in Dutch. (K. K. V.)

543

JOHANNES[5] VIELE, of Abraham,[4] Jacob,[3] Louwis,[2] Pieter Cornelisen[1],

bap. Mar. 20, 1774; m. Margaret Bradshaw. Children:

    636   Margaret Ann, b. May 26, 1804, d. June 28, 1808.

+637   William Bradshaw, b. Sep. 14, 1808, m. Celinda Boynton, d. Apr., 1837.

550

JACOB[5] VIELE, of Stephen,[4] Jacob,[3] Louwis,[2] Pieter Cornelisen[1], b. Jan. 30, 1774; m. ——. Children:

+638   Charles, b. ——.

"One of Jacob's sons, Charles Viele, lives at Wolcott, N. Y." (Letter of his cousin Jacob, son of Simon Toll Viele, to E. L. Viele, 1874.)

1800. Jacob S. (Stephen) Viele was witness to the will of his uncle, Ludovicus Viele, of Saratoga. (Fernow's Cal. of Wills.)

Jacob was left by his grandfather a farm in Saratoga Co., N. Y.

In 1818 Jacob and his son Charles, settled in Wayne Co., N. Y.

553

LUDOVICUS[5] VIELE, of Stephen,[4] Jacob,[3] Louwis,[2] Pieter Cornelisen[1],

b. Mar. 30, 1783; m. Hannah Pruyn. Children:

+639   Stephen, b. 1808, d. 1873; m. Jemima Waldron, b. July 27, 1812.

    640   Magdalena, b. 1810, d. 1859.

    641   Francis Pruyn, b. 1812, d. 1857.

    642   Sara Toll, b. 1814, d. 1895.

    643   Lewis Fort, b. 1816, d. 1820.

644   Abraham Pruyn, b. 1818, d. 1819.
645   Ellen M., b. 1820, d. 1898; m. Watson Sanford.

554

CAREL HANSEN[5] VIELE, of Stephen,[4] Jacob,[3] Louwis,[2] Pieter Cornelisen[1],

b. June 4, bap. Oct. 19, 1788; m. ——. Children:

646   Cornelis, b. ——.

"One of Charles' sons, Cornelis, lives near Red Creek, N.
Y." (Letter of Jacob Viele (cousin to Cornelis) written to
Gen. E. L. Viele, 1874.)

556

SIMON[5] TOLL VIELE, of Stephen,[4] Jacob,[3] Louwis,[2] Pieter Cornelisen[1],

b. ——; m. Zernah Hill.   Children:

+647   Stephen, b. 1803, m. 1st, Caroline Louise Lum; 2d,
       Catharine Mary Dewey, b. 1813, d. Nov. 27,
       1840; 3d, Helen Hasbrouck Buckingham, wid.
       of Capt. Henry Holden, b. June, 1812, d. May 20,
       1898.   He d. 1862.
647a   Sara, b. 1804.
648   Daniel, b. 1805.
648a   Hester, b. 1808.
649   Jacob, b. 1812.
649a   Eva M., b. 1815.
650   Simon, b. 1816.
650a   Alida, b. 1818.
651   Zernah, b. 1823, m. Robert Armstrong.

Jacob was alive in 1874.   On May 2 of that year he writes
to Gen. E. L. Viele from Seneca Falls, N. Y., but does not
mention his wife's name.   He speaks of his son but without giving his name.   He speaks of his cousin Stephen of Lansing-
burg, N. Y. (b. 1808) as older than himself.

Simon Viele is said to have gone as tutor into the family of a
planter in Columbus, Ga., and to have married his daughter.

Simon's niece, Mrs. Vickery, writes (Jan. 1910): "I remember him perfectly for he came to Seneca Falls to visit us when I was eighteen years old and brought with him his oldest daughter who was about my age, and named Leonora."

Mrs. Vickery also writes, "my father's (Stephen's) two brothers, Daniel and Jacob, were farmers."

564

JACOB[6] VIELE, of Johannes,[4] Jacob,[3] Louwis,[2] Pieter Cornelisen[1], b. Aug. 23, 1781; m. —— Martin. Children:

>   652 Rufus, b. ——.
>   653 William, b. ——.
>   654 Jane, b. ——.

565

MARIA[5] VIELE, of Johannes,[4] Jacob,[3] Louwis,[2] Pieter Cornelisen[1], b. Apr. 13, 1783; m. Hugh Groesbeck. Children (Groesbeck):

>   655 Catrina, b. Jan. 1, bap. Oct. 28, 1798, wit: Louis and Catrina Viele.

566

JOHN[5] J. VIELE, of Johannes,[4] Jacob,[3] Louwis,[2] Pieter Cornelisen[1], b. July 3, bap. July 6, 1786; m. Kathalina Pattison (b. Jan. 12, 1812) Nov. 14, 1827; d. Oct. 12, 1859. John J. Viele was 40 and Kathalina 16 at the time of their marriage. Children (all born in Saratoga):

>   656 Abram, b. Mar. 17, 1829, m. Cornelia K. Williams June 18, 1863, at N. Hempstead, L. I.
>   657 Maria, b. Mar. 23, 1831, d. May 1, 1834, at Saratoga.
>   658 Judith Ann, b. Feb. 4, 1833, m. John Marshall Sep. 15, 1858, at Saratoga.
> +659 James Pattison, b. Mar. 25, 1835, m. Hester Viele Sep. 6, 1864, at Ft. Miller, N. Y.
> +660 Catharine Maria, b. Aug. 9, 1837, m. Lorenzo P. Viele Oct. 16, 1860.
>   661 John J., b. Apr. 20, 1839, d. at Saratoga Aug. 28, 1896.

662 Harmon L., b. Apr. 23, 1841, m. Katharine F. Free-
man June 4, 1872, at Stillwater, N. Y., d. 1900.

663 Isaiah, b. Oct. 18, 1843, d. Oct. 7, 1853, at Saratoga.

664 Mary Elizabeth, b. Nov. 25, 1849, m. O. D. Kirk,
at Schuylersville, N. Y., Aug. 13, 1878.

It is said that Harmon Viele's farm was part of the original
grant to his grandfather in 1791, which included what is now
Saratoga Springs. Katharine F. Viele (wid. of Harmon L.)
writes from Saratoga Nov. 11, 1909, "I send you copy from
family Bible of three last generations."

568

NICHOLAS[5] VIELE, of Johannes,[4] Jacob,[3] Louwis,[2] Pieter Cornelisen[1],

b. June 28, bap. July 10, 1791; m. Sally Rogers. Children:

665 Maria, b. ——, m. D. van Antwerp.

666 John N., b. ——.

667 Catherina, b. ——.

668 Benjamin, b. ——.

669 Jane, b. ——.

670 Sara, b. ——.

671 Abraham, b. ——.

672 Cornelia, b. ——.

588

ANNA[6] VIELE, of Johannes,[5] Ludovicus,[4] Teunis,[3] Louwis,[2] Pieter
Cornelisen[1],

b. Oct. 12, 1794; m. David De Garmo. Children (De Garmo):

+673 William Ross, b. ——, m. Rhoda Wing Stewart.

607

LUDOVICUS[6] VIELE, of Simon T.,[5] Ludovicus,[4] Jacob,[3] Louwis,[2]
Pieter Cornelisen[1],

bap. Jan. 25, 1796; m. Laville Stearns Jan. 5, 1820, d. Nov. 26,
1882. Children:

674 Laville Stearns, b. Sep. 4, 1822, d. Jan. 5, 1894.
      Never married.
675 Elizabeth, b. Sep. 12, 1824.
676 Lewis, b. Sep. 24, 1826, m. Laura G. Ferris, of New
      York, Nov. 22, 1862. Lives in Chicago, Ill.
677 John, b. Jan. 23, 1828. Left home when young and
      was never afterwards heard from.
678 Oliver, b. Sep. 24, 1835, d. Mar. 24, 1837.
679 Laura Jane, b. Apr. 24, 1832. Lives in Marengo,
      Ohio.

608

PLATT CARPENTER[6] VIELE, of Simon,[5] Ludovicus,[4] Jacob,[3]
Louwis,[2] Pieter Cornelisen[1],
b. Aug. 16, 1797; m. Phoebe Bryan Nov. 15, 1820, d. Nov. 3,
1879, in Rochester, N. Y. Phœbe Bryan was b. June 2, 1801,
d. Jan. 27, 1881. Children:

680 Jane Elizabeth, b. Sep. 26, 1821, m. Wm. W. Bryan
      Oct. 17, 1837.
681 Frances Wickes, b. May 12, 1824, m. George Wash-
      burn Oct. 14, 1844, d. May 1, 1909.
682 Maria Bryan, b. Oct. 13, 1826, m. Charles H. Clark,
      Mar. 8, 1849. He d. Nov. 20, 1873.
683 Platt Bryan, b. Jan. 24, 1829, m. 1st, Julia M.
      Barton, May 26, 1859, who d. May 11, 1865; 2d,
      Olivia C. Chace, Dec. 22, 1881, who d. Apr. 15,
      1899. (Living and possessed of all his faculties
      at present date, Dec., 1909.)

610

JOHN CARPENTER[6] VIELE, of Simon,[5] Ludovicus,[4] Jacob,[3]
Louwis,[2] Pieter Cornelisen[1],
b. Apr. 20, 1806; m. Eliza Baker Oct. 31, 1832, d. Apr. 25, 1880.
Children:

684 Lorenzo Baker, b. Mar. 23, 1834, m. Catharine
      Viele Oct. 16, 1860, d. Feb. 5, 1880.
685 Jay, b. July 25, 1837, d. Jan. 29, 1842.

+686   Jane Eliza, b. Sep. 28, 1839, m. Alexander Stuart
         Dec. 10, 1863, d. Mar. 17, 1887.

687   Hester, b. Oct. 18, 1841, m. James Pattison Viele,
         Domine, Sep. 6, 1864, d. July 10, 1902.

+688   John Henry, b. Mar. 20, 1844, m. 1st, Lydia Amanda
         Wait, 1875; 2d, Martha Amelia Haxtun, of Ft.
         Edward, N. Y., 1881, d. at Ft. Miller, N. Y.,
         June 28, 1900.   John H. Viele was born and died
         in the Viele Homestead in Ft. Miller and was an
         Elder in the Dutch Ref. Church in that place.

689   Simon, b. May 18, 1851, d. Sep. 5, 1851.

John Carpenter is said to have purchased the Viele Homestead at Ft. Miller, N. Y., in 1836.   It is said to have been in
the family more than 100 years.   He was an Elder in the
Dutch Ref. Ch. in Ft. Miller as his son John was after him.

611

HIRAM[6] VIELE, of Simon,[5] Ludovicus,[4] Jacob,[3] Louwis,[2] Pieter
   Cornelisen[1],
   b. Sep. 5, 1813; m. Abby McFarland Oct. 17, 1838, d. July 25,
1874.   Children:

690   Mary Jane, b. Sep. 18, 1839, d. Sep. 19, 1840.
691   Henry Clarence, b. Oct. 29, 1841, m. Elizabeth F.
         Mack (b. May 20, 1842) on Oct. 16, 1873.   Lives
         in Akron, Ohio.
692   Mary Jane, b. Feb. 15, 1845.   Lives in Akron, Ohio.
693   Frances Gale, b. Mar. 30, 1847.
694   Charles Dana, b. Sep., 1849.

Hiram Viele, born in Pittstown, Rensselaer Co., N. Y.,
moved with his parents to Ft. Miller, N. Y.   In 1836 he went
to Rochester, N. Y., and in 1842 to Akron, Ohio.   In Akron
he had a large flour mill and feed store.

613

LUDOVICUS[6] VIELE, of Abraham,[5] Ludovicus,[4] Jacob,[3] Louwis,[2]
   Pieter Cornelisen[1],

b. Apr. 14, 1802; m. Caroline Eliza Hunt, of Johnsonville, N. Y. (sister of Judge Harmen P. Hunt), July 1, 1829, in Pittstown, N. Y. Married by Rev. Mark Tucker, of Troy. (C. E. Hunt was b. Mar. 4, 1810.) Children:

695　Louise Douglass, b. May 24, 1835, at Pittstown, N. Y., m. Gen. Jacob Gartner Lauman July 6, 1853, at Davenport, Iowa; married by the Rev. J. D. Mason; d. Feb. 4, 1900, at Chicago, Ill. Gen. Lauman was the son of George and Margaret Lauman. He was b. in Taneytown, Md., Jan. 20, 1813, brought up in York, Pa., went later to Burlington, Iowa, where he was first in general business and afterwards a banker. During the war of 1861 he was Brigadier and Brevet Major General, and d. Feb. 7, 1867, at Burlington, Iowa. (Descendants.)

696　Josephine Ludoveca, b. 1840, m. James Stafford Crew. Living at Berkeley, Cal., 1909. (Descendants.)

697　Augusta Paine, b. 1838, m. Dugald McMillan, d. Sep. 30, 1907.

Ludovicus had a cotton mill and store at Valley Falls, N. Y. He was a strong character and a man of consequence in his part of the country. He died of cholera at St. Louis, Mo., where he had gone on business during an epidemic of that disease. His grave could never be identified and his sister Patience erected a monument to his memory in the Newcomb lot in the cemetery at Davenport, Iowa.

616

WILLIAM DOUGLASS[6] VIELE, of Abraham,[5] Ludovicus,[4] Jacob,[3] Louwis,[2] Pieter Cornelisen[1],

b. 1808; m. Sarah M. Newcomb, d. July 19, 1866. Children:

698　Mary Hannah, b. 1835, m. Oliver Eckel.
699　Ellen Douglass, b. 1839, m. S. D. Palmer.
700　George C., b. 1843.
701　Margaret, b. 1846.

620

CHARLES[6] VIELE, of Abraham,[5] Ludovicus,[4] Jacob,[3] Louwis,[2] Pieter Cornelisen[1],

b. Nov. 22, 1818; m. Mary Jane Hopkins, dau. of Judge Edward Hopkins, Dec. 28, 1843; d. Sep. 23, 1901. Mary Jane Hopkins b. Jan. 10, 1824, d. Oct. 3, 1899.

Born in the Viele Homestead in Valley Falls, N. Y., Charles Viele studied at the Troy Academy and went into business at that place. Later he went into business at Saratoga Springs, and in 1836 he started for the West, and after a long and difficult journey arrived at Evansville, Ind., where he made his home and established himself as a succesful man of affairs. He was President and Director of the First National Bank of Evansville: director in various other institutions in that city, and vestryman in both the Episcopal churches. At the time Mr. Viele wrote a sketch of his life (1900) he was the only member of his own generation alive. Children:

702   George Bement, b. Oct. 16, 1847, m. Amy Morgan.

703   Mary Douglas, b. Sep. 12, 1850, d. Aug. 4, 1857.

704   Walter Stuart, b. Oct. 31, 1853, m. Margaret Winters; d. Oct. 23, 1906.

705   Charles Abram, b. Sep. 20, 1858, d. Apr. 5, 1867.

706   Edward Newcomb, b. June 8, 1860, m. Daisy Potter. (One son, Douglas, b. Apr. 21, 1891.)

626

STEPHEN D.[6] VIELE, of Stephen,[5] Ludovicus,[4] Jacob,[3] Louwis,[2] Pieter Cornelisen[1],

b. 1830, at Ft. Miller, N. Y., m. Martha Ann Shuler Nov. 24, 1857, d. Feb. 9, 1907, at the Nat. Military Home, Ohio. Children:

707   Evelyn Maria (Kitty) b. Oct. 9, 1858, m. John J. Everson Feb. 4, 1884.

708   Martha Ann (Daisy), b. Oct. 6, 1864, d. 1877.

LOUISA CAROLINE WINNE
(neé VIELE)

628

LOUISA CAROLINE[6] VIELE, of John L.,[5] Ludovicus,[4] Jacob,[3] Louwis,[2] Pieter Cornelisen[1],

b. May 18, 1812, in the Knickerbocker Homestead at Schaghticoke, N. Y.; m. Charles Winne, M.D., Sep. 30, 1836. Children (Winne):

711   Charles Knickerbocker, b. June 30, 1838, m. Caroline Elizabeth Frey Giddings Dec. 3, 1874. (Mrs. Winne is the great granddaughter of Major John Frey, a Revolutionary officer on the staff of Gen. Herkimer.)

712   Sarah Cathalina, b. 1846, d. 1849.

Charles Winne, b. Oct. 22, 1811, was the eldest son of Jellis Winne, Jr., and Sarah Fondey his wife, both of Albany, N. Y. He was educated at the Albany Academy, graduated from Union College, Schenectady, N. Y., and from the New York College for Physicians and Surgeons. After his graduation he settled in Buffalo, N. Y., and there, a wise and cultured physician, practised his profession till his death on May 9, 1877. (Vide Transactions Erie Co. Medical Society, Oct. 17, 1877.)

Charles Knickerbocker Winne was educated at the Albany Academy and graduated at the Jefferson Medical College in 1859. He entered the Medical Corps, U. S. Army, in 1861, and served with Gen. McClellan's column in West Virginia. He joined the Army of the Potomac in Sep. 1863, serving therein as Surgeon in Chief and subsequently Medical Inspector of the 5th Corps until the army was disbanded July 1, 1865, in Washington. He was present at the following engagements: Rich Mountain, West Va.; Rappahannock Station and Mine Run; the Wilderness, Spottsylvania, North Anna; Cold Harbor, Assault and Siege of Petersburg; Weldon Railroad, Hutcher's Run, Quaker Road, White Oak Ridge, Five Forks. He engaged in the pursuit of Lee and the surrender at Appomattox Court House, being one of the ten surviving officers (1909) who were present in the court yard while the terms of surrender were being considered by Generals Grant and

Lee. He was brevetted Captain and Major for "faithful and meritorious services" during the war, and brevetted Lieut. Col. for "meritorious and distinguished services" at Tybee Island, Ga., where cholera prevailed. In 1875 Col. Winne was offered a commission as Lieut. Col. on the Medical Staff of the Army of Egypt. He was retired for age June 30, 1902, as Lieut. Col. and Deputy Surgeon General U. S. A. Promoted as "Col. U. S. A., Retired" by Act of Congress Apr. 23, 1904. He holds the government bronze medal for the campaigns of the Civil War; is a member of the Military Order of the Loyal Legion, Sons of the American Revolution, and of the Holland Society. Col. Winne has one son, Charles Winne, M.D., of Albany, N. Y.

629

RUFUS KING[6] VIELE, of John L.,[5] Ludovicus,[4] Jacob,[3] Louwis,[2] Pieter Cornelisen[1],
    b. Dec. 3, 1813; m. Phebe Ann Gregory May 18, 1840, d. Dec. 22, 1891. Phebe Ann Gregory b. Mar. 27, 1817, d. Jan. 14, 1892. Children:

> 713   Charles Delavan, b. Feb. 8, 1841, m. Nannie D. Minor, Jan. 10, 1873. No children.
> 714   Mary Cathalina, b. July 11, 1844, m. Talbot Olyphant, Apr. 27, 1865. (Four daughters.)

Talbot Olyphant is President (1909) of the N. Y. Society of the Cincinnati.

> 715   Lois Marion, b. Aug. 13, 1847, d. Jan. 30, 1898. Unmarried.

Charles Delavan Viele was commissioned 2d Lieut 1st Infantry, U. S. A., in which regiment his uncle Egbert Ludovicus Viele also served. In active service during the Civil War and on Apr. 22, 1868, he reached the rank of Captain. On the reorganization of the Army he was on Jan. 1, 1871, assigned to the 10th Cavalry, and remained in it till Aug. 20, 1899, when he received his commission as Major. He was then assigned to the 1st Cavalry and was commissioned Lieut. Col. of the same regiment Nov. 21, 1897. Sep. 14, 1899, he was commissioned Col. of the 4th Cavalry, U. S. A., and retired for disability Jan. 23, 1900. For Civil War service he was promoted Brigadier General (retired) Apr. 23, 1904. He resides in Los Angeles, Cal.

630

AUGUSTUS[6] VIELE, M.D., of John L.,[5] Ludovicus,[4] Jacob,[3] Louwis,[2] Pieter Cornelisen[1],

b. Sep. 5, 1815; m. Mary Kenyon, of Herkimer, N. Y., Oct. 8, 1839, d. Feb. 12, 1882. Children:

716 Kenyon Griswold, b. Sep. 29, 1840, m. Helen R. Bucknam, Oct. 7, 1874 (three children.)

717 Augustus Hamilton, b. Nov. 10, 1843, m. Mary Stuart Feb. 12, 1865. She was b. Sep. 27, 1845, d. Dec. 28, 1898, and was the dau. of Gen. Geo. Beebe Stuart and Frances Neeles. (Two sons.)

718 Mary Adela, b. Sep. 6, 1845, m. Willis H. Brumley Nov. 19, 1868. (One son.)

719 Helen K., b. Jan. 11, 1856, m. 1st, George Welles Perkins, June 12, 1877; 2d, Edward Tatum, Apr. 27, 1885. (Three daughters.)

Augustus Viele was an excellent physician and practised his profession for years in Troy, N. Y. Later he came to New York City where he practised and was a member of the Board of Health. Some 35 years ago the compiler stood by the bed of an aged woman in St. Luke's Hospital, N. Y., who, on hearing her name, exclaimed: "I bless the name of Viele!" She had been a patient of Dr. Viele's.

632

HENRY KNICKERBOCKER[6] VIELE, of John L.,[5] Ludovicus,[4] Jacob,[3] Louwis,[2] Pieter Cornelisen[1],

b. Apr. 29, 1819; m. Letitia P. Thompson Aug. 15, 1843, d. Aug. 8, 1881. Educated in the Albany Academy where in 1836 he took the Caldwell Prize for Mathematics. (Mun. An.,

Vol. II, p. 320.) He made the law his profession and in 1863 was Col. of the 94th N. Y. Volunteers.   Children:

720   John Ludovicus, b. ——, d. in infancy.
721   Sheldon Thompson, b. Jan. 4, 1847, m. Anna Porter Dorr June 5, 1875. (Descendants.) Sheldon Thompson Viele graduated from Yale University A. B. 1868, and has since practised law in Buf‑ falo, N. Y. He was appointed by Gov. Higgins June, 1906, State Commissioner in Lunacy and reappointed March, 1907, by Gov. Hughes.

635

EGBERT LUDOVICUS[6] VIELE, of John L.,[5] Ludovicus,[4] Jacob,[3] Louwis,[2] Pieter Cornelisen[1],
b. June 17, 1825; m. 1st, Teresa Griffin, June 3, 1850; 2d, Juli‑ ette Henrietta Dana June 10, 1872, d. Apr. 22, 1902. (See Appendix.)   Children of Egbert L. Viele and Teresa Griffin:

722   Francis Griffin, b. Sep. 1, 1851, d. at Ringgold Bar‑ racks, Texas, Mar. 27, 1852. ("Bosey.")
723   Kathlyne Knickerbocker, b. Jan. 12, 1853, at New Brighton, Staten Island, N. Y. Never married.
724   Herman Knickerbocker, b. Jan. 31, 1856, in New York City, m. Mary Ashhurst Wharton Sep. 1, 1887, at Washington, D. C., d. in New York City Dec. 14, 1908. (See Appendix.)
725   Francis Griffin, b. and d. in New York City on June 8, 1857.
726   Teresa, b. Oct. 12, 1858, in New York City, d. Aug. 11, 1879, in New York City. ("Tesa.") Never married.
727   Mary Violette, b. Apr. 26, 1862, d. Nov. 29, 1862. Born and d. in New York City.
728   Egbert L., Jr. (who took the name of Francis Viele‑ Griffin), b. Apr. 23, 1863, at Norfolk, Va. (while his father was Military Governor of that city), m. Marie Brockli in Paris, France. (Four

daughters, all b. and living in France.) (See Appendix.)

729 Emily, b. Mar. 18, 1865, m. Thomas Nelson Strother May 22, 1889, at Washington, D. C. Lives in Baltimore, Md. (Four daughters, three living.)

Teresa Griffin, b. Jan. 27, 1831, was the dau. of Francis Griffin, a much respected New York lawyer, d. 1852, and Mary Sands his wife. Teresa Griffin's grandfathers were George Griffin, a distinguished New York lawyer (called by David Dudley Field "the Nestor of the New York Bar" of his day): and Joseph Sands, partner in the old banking house of Ward, King & Sands, of New York, in the last century. Her great-grandfathers were Col. Zebulon Butler, a Continental officer, friend of Washington, an original member of the Order of the Cincinnati, and hero of the Wyoming Massacre, July 3, 1778, and Comfort Sands, one of the Committee of One Hundred chosen by the citizens of New York City to govern the city at the time of the Revolution, later President of the Chamber of Commerce, New York. Her ancestors were the founders of the following towns: 1637, New Haven (Wm. Peck); Old Lyme, (Joseph Peck); 1659, Norwich (Wm. and Sam Hyde), all in Connecticut; 1630, Roxbury (Dr. George Alcock); 1630, Charlestown (Dr. Richard Palgrave), in Massachusetts; also of Block Island (James Sands, Tristram Dodge, Robert Guthrie, Simon Ray); in 1683, of Southold. L. I. (Jasper Griffing), and in 1663, of West Farms, N. Y. (Edward Jessup). Among her ancestors were Mathew Griswald, of Massachusetts; Thomas Hunt, of Hunt's Point, N. Y.; Thomas Cornell, of Cornell's Neck, L. I.; Henry Wolcott and Edward Dorr, of Massachusetts.

637

WILLIAM BRADSHAW[6] VIELE, of Johannes,[5] Abraham,[4] Jacob,[3] Louwis,[2] Pieter Cornelisen[1],

b. Sep. 14, 1808, d. Apr. 1877; m. Celinda Boynton, b. Aug. 11, 1811, d. May 30, 1888. Children:

730   Eugene, b. Nov. 30, 1834, m. Mary J. Blodgett Mar.
14, 1867, d. Nov. 22, 1889.

Eugene Viele was a young man when the War of 1861 occurred. He "enlisted from Hinesburg, Vt., in Co. F, 9th Vermont Volunteers, and was commissioned 1st Lieut. June 25,
1852; promoted captain Co. I, 9th Vermont, and commissioned
Dec. 22, 1863; mustered out of the service of the U. S. June 13,
1865." He was in many battles; on the 15th of September,
1863, he was captured with his Regiment at Harper's Ferry,
and sent prisoner to Chicago, Ill., as paroled prisoner, but on
January 10, 1864, he was exchanged. He was with Gen.
Keyes in the Peninsula campaign and with the Army of the
Potomac in front of Petersburg, and engaged in the terrific battles about Ft. Harrison, Va., in Sep. 1864. On the morning of
Apr. 3, 1865, Capt. Viele was present with his command at the
capture of the city of Richmond. He had been detailed in the
fall of 1864 as ordnance officer of the 25th Army Corps (Maj.
Gen. Weitzel commanding), and he took one of the first ordnance trains into Richmond after its capture. Theo. S. Peck,
of Burlington, Vt., who was one of his comrades, says in a letter to his widow dated Nov. 19, 1909: "He was a good soldier,
fearless and courageous, a thorough gentleman and a noble
man." He was said to have been one of the best ordnance
officers in the Army of the James. He received an injury to
his leg by his horse falling on him, which, although it did not
incapacitate him at the time, produced results which caused his
death. (He left one daughter.)

731   Mary C., b. Apr. 30, 1836, m. Leonard Andrews.
732   Jane Bradshaw, b. Aug. 30, 1839, m. Henry T. Bene-
dict Feb. 3, 1867. Lives in Montreal, Canada.

William Bradshaw Viele left Schaghticoke early and settled
in Vermont where he married. His mother, Margaret Bradshaw, was the dau. of William Bradshaw and Sarah MacKil-
lips, of Schaghticoke, who m. Feb. 7, 1765. Margaret was
born Apr. 12, 1771, and d. July 13, 1819. Her brother, John
Bradshaw, of Schaghticoke, m. Rebecca Knickerbocker, Aug.
5, 1792. (N. Y. Gen. and Biog. Rec., Vol. XXXIX, p. 279.)

Mary J. Blodgett, wife of Eugene Viele, is the dau. of Luther Palmer Blodgett and Permelia Chittenden. Her grandmother was the dau. of Judge Truman Chittenden and granddaughter of the Hon. Thomas Chittenden, first Governor of Vermont. (Information from Mrs. Eugene Viele.)

638

CHARLES[6] VIELE, of Jacob,[5] Stephen,[4] Jacob,[3] Louwis,[2] Pieter Cornelisen[1],

b. ——, m. ——. Children:

    732b Charles W., b. ——. Lives at South Butler, N. Y.

639

STEPHEN[6] VIELE, of Ludovicus,[5] Stephen,[4] Jacob,[3] Louwis,[2] Pieter Cornelisen[1],

b. 1808; m. Jemima Waldron, b. July 27, 1812, and d. 1873. Children:

    733 Hannah L., b. ——, m. William Gordon.
    734 Margaret Jane, b. ——, m. 1st, John Lewis; 2d, John C. House.
    735 Hattie Newell, b. ——, m. Edgar C. Cole, M.D., d. Apr. 13, 1868.
    736 Sarah, b. ——, m. Frederick Blake.
    737 Stephen Theodore, b. 1849, m. Martha A. Brown, d. 1896. (Deed in N. Y. State Indexes of Martha A. Viele, wife of Theodore S.

See Riker's History of Harlem for Waldron family, p. 738. Deed of Jemima, wife of Stephen Viele, recorded in Albany Co., 1854. (N. Y. State Indexes.)

647

STEPHEN S.[6] VIELE, of Simon,[5] Stephen,[4] Jacob,[3] Louwis,[2] Pieter Cornelisen[1],

b. 1803; m. 1st, Caroline Louise Lum; 2d, Catharine Mary Dewey, b. 1813, d. Nov. 27, 1840; 3d, Helen Hasbrouck Buck-

ingham, wid. of Capt. Henry Holden, who d. 1839. She was
b. at Highland Falls, N. Y., June 2, 1812, d. at Ft. Atkinson,
Wis., May 20, 1898. Stephen S. d. 1862, at Seneca Falls,
N. Y. Children of Caroline Louise Lum:

738   Josephine, now dead (1909.)
739   Luther Fulton Stephen, now dead (1909.)

Children of Stephen S. Viele and Catharine Mary Dewey:

740   Caroline Mary, b. 1837, m. S. D. Vickery.
741   Edwin Whitney, b. ——.

Children of Stephen S. Viele and Helen Hasbrouck Bucking-
ham (wid. of Capt. Henry Holden):

741a Edward Mynderse, b. ——, d. 1894, in Chicago, Ill.
741b Henry Stephen, b. ——.
741c Helen Johanna, b. ——, d. 1877, in Oshkosh.
741d John Morgan, b. Feb. 18, 1851, at Seneca Falls,
        N. Y.; m. Margaret Kiels, b. N. Y. City Nov. 25,
        1852. Lives at Ft. Atkinson, Wis.

Information through Mrs. Vickery and John Morgan Viele.

686

JANE ELIZA[7] VIELE, of John C.,[6] Simon,[5] Ludovicus,[4] Jacob,[3]
        Louwis,[2] Pieter Cornelisen[1],
    b. Sep. 28, 1839; m. Alexander Stuart Dec. 10, 1863, d. Mar.
17, 1887. Children:

742   Henry Clarence Stuart, of Ft. Miller, N. Y., b. Feb.
        22, 1865; m. Serena De Garmo, dau. of William
        R. De Garmo, and granddaughter of Anne Viele,
        dau. of John L. Viele, of Schaghticoke, N. Y.
        H. C. Stuart is Chief Clerk of Customs and Spe-
        cial Deputy Collector in the N. Y. Custom House
        (1909).

1690. Jeremy Viele and Ann his wife, on Long Island. Nothing connects them with this family.

1700. Dec. 12, David Vielie, and on Oct. 3, 1702, Johannes Viele witness wills in N. Y.

1701. Lawrence Claas Viele demands pay as interpreter to the Indians and for sweeping chimneys at Ft. Ann. (Col. Doc., Vol. IV, p. 891.) This name appears three times and twice without the "Viele." It may have been a mistake to have added Viele.

1703. Stephen Viele is mentioned in the Kingston church records as witness at the baptism of a child of Adam Swart—again as witness for a child of Arent Vynhout and Marytje Viele, (dau. of Pieter Cornelisen Viele). Once more, in 1704, as witness for a child together with Pieternella Viele (dau. of Pieter Cornelisen Viele). He must have been connected with the Pieter Cornelisen branch of the family as he is associated with the Swarts, with Marytje and Pieternella Viele and bears the name of Stephen, a name only found in that branch and in that very often. The phrase used by Pearson in connection with Louwis Viele, "only surviving son" (of Pieter) and seeming to be from a deed prevents Stephen from being certainly ascribed to Pieter Cornelisen as a son.

1697. Lisbet Aroutse Viele, otherwise called Lisbet Aroutse V. Eli. She appears to have married Gerrit Jacobs and to have had at least two children (Meesje and Cornelis). Gerrit Jacobs in 1699 takes the oath at Kinderhook, and on April 6, 1699, Lysbet Viele is admitted a member of the church at Kinderhook, and after her name is written "died Neoborocum" meaning in New York. MacMurray thinks she is the same Lisbet whom I have written in as dau. of Pieter Cornelisen—this may be, but the record is too vague to assign her a place. Her name of Lysbet Arentse would assign her to Arnout as a daughter, but she seems to have no connection with that family. I place her here for future study.

1733. William Viele is witness at a Kingston baptism.

1740. Peter van Deusen and Cornelia Viele his huys vroouw witnesses at baptism.

1742. Joel, child of Jeremia du Bois and Rachel Vielen.

1749. Nov. 22, Patrick, child of Patrick Flat and Eliner Viele, witnesses: John and Rachel de Peyster.

1760. Joseph Viele, of Dutchess Co., has not received his pension.

1753. Aug. 1, Catharine Viele and Daniel Higgins (N. Y. Mar.)

1760. July 20, Nicholas Viel and Martha Rogers (N. Y. Mar.)

1769. Rachel Vielle and Henry Staats. (N. Y. Mar.)

1770. Simeon Viele and Neeltje Palmetier; children born: Cornelis, b. Apr. 30, 1777; Ariaantje, b. 1779.

1764. Ann Vielle and Joseph Pierson. (N. Y. Mar.)

1788. Feb. 3, Margaret, child of Maria Vielen and Turk (Dirck) Krom, wit: John Krom and Margarietta Filen. There is a Dirck Krom in Ulster Co., in 1728, son of Floris Krom. Maria is evidently a granddaughter of Philip, but the link is missing. Floris Krom had patent where Haverstraw now is.

1782. Susannah Veil and Jacob Brush.

1792. Hendrickje, child of John van Arnhem and Sally Viele. (Schaghticoke.)

1800. Stephen Viele, m. Mary (Polly) Abbott Jan. 23, child Rachel b. Sep. 23, 1800. Schaghticoke Rec.).

And others.

617

DELIA MARIA[6] VIELE, of Abraham,[5] Ludovicus,[4] Jacob,[3] Louwis,[2] Pieter Cornelisen,[1]

b. Mar. 28, 1810; m. David Rorer Mar. 21, 1839; d. Nov. 4, 1888. David Rorer b. in Pittsylvania Co., Va., May 12, 1806; d. July 7, 1884. He stood at the head of the Iowa Bar and was for 26 years Attorney for the C. B. and Q. R. R. He wrote several valuable books on Law. Children (Rorer):

701a Virginia Douglas, b. Apr. 3, 1842, d. Apr. 27, 1898. "A woman of such charm and so dearly loved that her birthday is still observed by her friends."

701b Delia Maria, b. Oct. 28, 1844.

701c Mary Louisa, b. Sept. 19, 1849, m. John Terry Remey Oct. 30, 1872. (One son, David Rorer Remey, b. July 11, 1878, d. Apr. 27, 1902.)

Miss D. M. Rorer writes from Burlington, Iowa: "My grandfather, Abraham Viele, was born at 'the Valley,' now Valley Falls, in Pittstown, Rensselaer Co., N. Y., Oct. 8, 1772. He married Hannah, daughter of Samuel Douglas and Patience Ferguson his wife, June 21, 1796. Abraham had a cotton mill at Valley Falls, but for a short time lived at what was called the State Line House, near Bennington, Vt. While there, about 1820, Aaron Burr visited a neighbor, who brought him to call at the Viele home. Grandmother remained in a sitting room on one side of the hall and refused to see the unwelcome guest, but allowed my mother to carry in the snuffers tray to the parlor opposite. My mother was but 10 years old, but she never forgot Burr's piercing black eyes. My grandfather came out to what is now Iowa in 1837, settled and died here. I have a satinwood desk that belonged to our mutual great grandmother, Eva Toll. It came to me seven years ago from the descendants of my great aunt, Jane Carpenter Viele. My mother has often told me that during the Revolutionary war, while her husband, Ludovicus Viele, was in the army, Eva Toll, seeing an Indian in the distance from her garden and having been warned by friends of the untrust-worthiness of a man slave, became alarmed lest the Indians, instigated by the British, were about to make a descent upon the village, took her children, and with such of her posses-sions as she could put in bed-tickings and carry on the backs of horses, fled in the night from Valley Falls and sought refuge in Albany, where there was a fort."

ERRATA

PAGE 19, line 15. Claverrick should read Claverrock.

PAGE 34, line 28. Cornelia should read Cornelis.

PAGE 35, line 27. Bont should read Bout.

PAGE 36, line 25. Segars should read Segers.

PAGE 38, line 15. Stephn should read Stephen.

PAGE 42, line 21. Mar. 2 should read Mar. 21.

PAGE 56, line 24. (No. 136) second "b." should read "m."

PAGE 56, line 24. Archabild should read Archibald.

PAGE 58, line 21. Sotter should read Satterlee.

PAGE 64, line 4. Pierson should read Pearson.

PAGE 65, line 34. Gysling should read Gyseling.

PAGE 68, lines 16 and 24. Gysling should read Gyseling.

PAGE 66, line 19. Roberts should read Robert.

PAGE 88, line 34. Barber should read Barbar.

PAGE 97, line 14. Zernah should read Zeruah.

PAGE 108, line 4. Zernah should read Zeruah.

PAGE 105, line 24. For June read May.

PAGE 121, line 10. For Charles W., read Lucien H.

APPENDIX

1. GENERAL EGBERT LUDOVICUS VIELE.

2. HERMAN KNICKERBOCKER VIELE.

3. EGBERT L. VIELE, JR. (known as Francis Viele-Griffin.)

4. VIELES: Elders and Deacons in the Dutch Church at Schaghticoke, N. Y., 1763–98.

Egbert L Viele

GENERAL EGBERT LUDOVICUS VIELE

WRITTEN BY RICHARD HENRY SAVAGE SEVERAL YEARS BEFORE THE
DEATH OF GEN. VIELE.

Few men are living to-day in New York City who link together
the historic New York, the vanished New York of the fifties—
and the Greater New York of to-day. Prominent among these
honored citizens is General Egbert L. Viele, whose beautiful home
on Riverside Drive attests his cultured tastes and travelled experience. It is given to few men to have played a conspicuous part
in the history of the great city of his choice, and in the national
service; to have succeeded in both civil and military life. It
fills up the measure of honor for a soldier to have served in a
series of three great wars, our Mexican war, our Indian campaign and the long Slavery contest begun in '61. General Viele's
family descent represents the historic New York. His birth and
military education both ally him to that State: while his services
as soldier, scientist and Congressman form a bright page in our
national records; and his professional labors and travels unite
him with many learned societies at home and abroad, making his
fifty years of effective manhood the record of a versatile and well-
spent life. He was on the roll of members of the Association of
Graduates of West Point, the Grand Army, the Loyal Legion, the
Century and New York clubs, the Union League, the St. Nicholas, the Aztec, the Holland Society, the National Academy, and
the Geographical and Genealogical Societies.

The eminent soldier-engineer was born in the home of his
father, the Hon. John L. Viele, in Waterford, N. Y. In an old
Dutch Bible now in the possession of his nephew, Charles Knickerbocker Winne, his mother's name is recorded as Kathlyne
Knickerbocker, whose family name the gifted Irving has made a
wide-world spell.

When Lieutenant Viele was graduated at West Point in 1847,
he had been the classmate there of many of the foremost leaders
in our Civil War. As an officer of the First Infantry, United
States Army, under Generals Scott and Taylor, he rapidly made
his mark; serving also with the First Dragoons. In the leisure

of five years' romantic service in Texas and the far West, he extended his professional studies and after being military governor of Laredo, Texas, he resigned to enter upon a cosmopolitan career of practical and consulting engineering, in which he has been eminently successful. In 1859, impelled by his personal experience during virulent epidemics of cholera and yellow fever, while he was a boy commander on the Southwest frontier, he began an active crusade in New York City in behalf of sanitary reform. Aided by well-known members of the medical profession he took the lead, backed by rare powers of oratory, and undisputable scientific analysis, and paved the way for those important measures that have resulted in establishing Boards of Health in nearly every town, city and State, as well as a National Board, whose paternal care now watches over the health and lives of more than seventy millions of people. He conceived and executed a topographical atlas of the city of New York which is at once a guide to the medical profession and a protest against that conflict between art and nature in public improvements whereby the laws of health are violated. This atlas alone is a scientific monument of which any man might be proud. His talents won for him the position of chief engineer of Central Park, New York, and Prospect Park, Brooklyn. These two monuments, dressed in living green, should perpetuate his memory. He responded to the first call for volunteers in 1861, and as captain of Co. K, of the 7th New York, commanded the detachment of that Regiment which, on the steamer "Daylight," opened the Potomac to Washington. He was rapidly advanced, being commissioned Brigadier General of Volunteers on Aug. 17, 1861. He led his troops to victory at Ft. Pulaski, participating in the capture of Norfolk. His services at Port Royal and in opening the Potomac were noteworthy and he was until October, 1863, Military Governor of Norfolk. After the war General Viele lent himself to many financial and engineering enterprises, including the projection of the elevated railways and cable systems of New York City. His record as a Congressman from the 13th District in 1885 is an honorable and useful one, his labors for the Harlem Ship Canal being especially marked.

The general's services as Commissioner and President of the Department of Public Parks mark an honorable rounding out of his first labors for the project of promoting breathing places for the people. In 1886 this old soldier was a Congressional member of the Board of Visitors at West Point, and his report for that year is a model of erudition and clearness—some well-devised reforms following in the wake of his suggestions therein made.

General Viele is the author of "Viele's Handbook of Active Service," and of many valuable monographs and reports. The Confederates complimented him by reprinting his handbook, turning its practical suggestions very neatly against the Federal side. The blue books of the House of Lords record the honors extended to General Viele by a special committee of fifteen peers, in 1895, when the Duke of Norfolk, Marquis of Salisbury, Earl of Denbigh, Lord Zouche, Earl Dunraven, Lord Halsbury and others, specially invited him as an expert representative American engineer and publicist, to advise them upon municipal improvements and laws concerning them in America. A luncheon with the above named gentlemen and a visit to the Duke of York at St. James Palace followed these conferences.

The distinguished veteran whose life is herein sketched has nobly returned to his State and country the trust of his public education at the West Point Military Academy, and the success of his life was no doubt in great part due to the discipline of "Old Army days" which aided in the development of his native force of character.

*　　*　　*　　*　　*　　*　　*

In 1902 General Viele died quite suddenly: indeed, he was taken ill while attending a dinner of the 7th Regiment Veterans, and was scarcely in his own house when the end came. During his last years he was much taken up, as Mr. Savage has said, with West Point interests, and he erected in the Military Cemetery at that place his own tomb, to which he was borne in the latter part of April, 1902, with military honors.　　　　K. K. V.

HERMAN KNICKERBOCKER VIELE

Herman Knickerbocker Viele was born in New York City on January 31, 1856, in a house on Fourth Avenue, near 20th Street, opposite the brick and marble Unitarian Church,—called at times by reason of its striped appearance—the church of the Zebra, and he died in December, 1908, at the Hotel Le Marquis scarcely a half-mile from the place of his birth.

The fifty odd years that marked the period of his life saw many changes in the metropolis, but they saw no change in the loyalty of this citizen to whom New York with its multitudinous interests was emphatically home. The life of the big city satisfied him, and the motto of one of his books—"give me faces and streets"—expresses his own attitude.

Possessed of an extremely sensitive temperament, to which was united a keen intelligence, it may well be said that his response to life conditions wore him out. In all that he did he was wont to throw himself with overmuch earnestness. He was happy in the mental gifts which enabled him to disclose himself to his fellowmen as he has in the three or four sprightly novels which have afforded, and which still afford, delight to many readers by their wit, their delicate fantasy and their excellent character drawing as well as in some very charming poetry.

In 1900 Herman K. Viele published his first book—"The Inn of the Silver Moon." This has been well called "a thistledown romance," for the reader pursues the tale page after page eagerly— as though racing after a veritable thistledown over a breezy moor, and when the end is reached one is possessed of a bright, ephemeral illusive, impression—thistledown in character—and the blood is tingling with the delight which comes from an absorbing interest.

Of this book his friend, Thomas A. Janvier, writes in his introduction to a volume of short stories of Herman K. Viele's published since his decease:—"Viele delighted in creating delightfully fantastic conditions lightly bordering upon the impossible: and having created them in so dissolving their elements into the seemingly commonplace and apparently probable, that the fine art with

which he worked his transmutation was veiled by the very per-
fection of its accomplishment. Such was the method which he
employed in what I cherish as his masterpiece:—"The Inn of the
Silver Moon"—a story told so simply and so directly and with
such a color of engaging frankness, that each turn in its series of
airily adjusted situations leaves upon the mind of the reader a
lasting impression of verity."

H. K. Viele in his second story, "The Last of the Knickerbockers,"—paints a picture of a phase of New York life which is none
the less true because it has not hitherto been recognized, and deals
with the gradual passing away of social conditions once predomi-
nating that reminds one of Hawthorne's presentment of the Pyn-
chons in "The House of the Seven Gables." My brother has introduced names of his own dead and gone ancestors into this book
although under circumstances quite imaginary. Alida de Wan-
dalear was the sister of his ancestor, Johannes de Wandalaer,
Deacon of Albany's Dutch church in 1690. Toll, Schepmoes,
Groesbeck and Van Epps are some of these names.

Mr. Janvier says of this, "Last of the Knickerbockers"—"It is
a good story to read simply as a story: but it is more than that,
it is a document: an ambered preservation of a phase of New
York society that already almost has vanished, and that soon will
have vanished absolutely. So true a presentment as this story of
New York's old time straight faiths and straighter social cus-
tims will outlive long, I am confident, the great mass of the fiction
of Viele's day. It will be actively alive while even a faint memory of these faiths and customs is cherished by living people and
when all such ancients shall have retired (with the final befitting
dignity attendant upon a special license) to their family homes
beneath the shadow of St. Mark's and of Trinity, carrying their
memories with them, it will become, as I have said, a document
preserving the traditions which otherwise would have been buried
with them and so linking permanently as they linked temporarily
—New York's ever-increasing ardent present with its never-pall-
ing less strenuous past."

Other books of H. K. Viele's are "Myra of the Pines," an
amusing romance, the scene of which is agreeably laid in the New
Jersey pine belt; "Heart Break Hill,"—his last—and a collection
of some of his poems published under the title of "Random

Verse." Of these last many are charming, and one, "In Saecula Saeculorum," is beautiful.

Since his death a collection of short stories has been published under the title, "On the Lightship," and edited by his friend, Thomas A. Janvier, from whose introduction to that collection these quotations have been made. I have spoken first of his writings although his books were the accomplishment of his later years. He began his career as a civil engineer, following in this his father's lead. Partly to establish his health—never very robust—and fired in part, no doubt, by love of adventure, he went out in the early seventies to the Rocky Mountains and practised his profession in Leadville then just budding out from a mining camp into a city of mushroom growth. Later he returned to the East and for two years worked on the West Shore road, then building. During this time he was stationed at Kingston, where he made many warm friends.

About 1885 he went to Washington and was engaged in developing the new part of the capitol city when his health broke down and he was forced to lay aside business. In 1887 he had married Miss Mary A. Wharton, daughter of Dr. Francis Wharton, of Philadelphia, as well known in early life as a professor of divinity as he was later as a jurist and an exponent of International Law. To recruit his health, Mr. Viele travelled extensively in Europe with his wife, and while there devoted much time to painting for which he had always shown a talent. In Paris he studied in the private atelier of Gabriel Ferrier. On his return from abroad Mr. Viele devoted his leisure to the cultivation of this talent. While yet a business man in Washington he had had his studio. His conception of painting was in line with the school of impressionism. One of his most striking pictures is "Sixth Ave. (N. Y.) on a Foggy Night"—a glimpse of the elevated with the red light of a train far above the street, the figure of a woman silhouetted against the circular glare of an electric light and a cab driving off in the grey distance and, overhanging all, pervading all, the fog itself half revealing, half concealing the scene and giving to it faint suggestions of mystery. In 1885 he exhibited in the Washington Society of Artists and two of his pictures, "Evening on Lake Como" and "Upper Broadway"—a study of the night lights of New York—were most favorably commented on. A year or so later he held an exhibition of his own pictures in Washington which was in every way a success. Coming soon after to New York (where he ever after lived) he painted on for a few years and then gave himself up almost exclusively to literature. My brother was associated during the years of his residence in New York with many of the cleverest writers of the day. Janvier, Brander Matthews, Booth Tarkington, and others. He belonged to the Century, Union, Salmagundi, Players, and other clubs, and was a Son of the Revolution, member of the St. Nicholas Society, of the Aztec and of the Genealogical Society. It was the exigency of the work he did for publication that caused him to lay aside the revising of his father's family chart—for his sister to complete. K. K. V.

BORDERLAND.

And have you been to Borderland?
Its country lies on either hand
    Across the river I-forget.
One crosses by a single stone—
So narrow one must cross alone,
    And all around its waters fret
    The laughing river I-forget.

Beneath the trees of Borderland,
One seems to know and understand,
    Across the river I-forget,
All languages of men and birds,
And all the sweet unspoken words
    One ever missed are murmured yet
    By that kind river I-forget.

Some day together hand and hand,
I'll take you there to Borderland,
    Beyond the river I-forget.
Some day when all our dreams come true—
One kiss for me and one for you—
    We'll watch the red sun sink and set
    Across the river I-forget.

                H. K. V.

EGBERT L. VIELE, JR.

KNOWN AS FRANCIS VIELE-GRIFFIN.

Egbert L. Viele, Jr., went with his mother to France when only nine years of age and has remained there ever since, marrying a Frenchwoman. He was educated in the foremost educational institutions of Paris, notably the College of St. Stanislaus—carrying off in one year as many as eleven prizes. As he grew older he assumed the name of his maternal grandfather in addition to his father's surname. He was born in Norfolk, Va., in April, 1863, while his father was Military Governor of that city. Viele-Griffin is virtually a Frenchman and has devoted his life to the career of literateur and journalist. He is one of the few Americans who has received for his poetry the ribbon of the Legion of Honor. He is editor of the "Mercure de France," a periodical founded in 1672, which was once conducted by Marmontel, and is now the exponent of all that is modern in thought and art. Extracts from an article on Viele-Griffin and his work by "M. A. V.," once printed in the *N. Y. Evening Post*, will no doubt be of interest to all who claim relationship with this talented man, and are as follows:—

"The French reviews recently noticed the new volume of poems by M. Francis Viele-Griffin, *Phocas le Jardinier*.

Its title page bears the imprint of the Societe du Mercure de France, which in itself indicates that the poems are of the new school of versification and of that mode of thought which is vaguely termed 'symbolistic,' but the nationality of the author should claim transatlantic comment. M. Francis Viele-Griffin is an American by birth and parentage and occupies a distinctive place in modern French literature.

When Viele-Griffin's first volume of poems was published in 1885, the critics detected at once a new accent, a clearness and sonorousness as yet uneven, with very marked qualities of rhythm. "Les Cygnes," which followed in 1887, was warmly received by the masters of modern French verse, Verlaine and Mallarmé. This volume contains a short idyll, "Le Porcher," which has been placed high among his work, and, indeed, pronounced unique in its way in French poetic literature. "Joies," which followed in 1889, first shows that skillful use of the old French ballad refrain which has become an admired characteristic of his lyrical style. Whether in these short poems or in the "Chavauchée d'Yeldis," a narrative of some length, or in the *fabliau* of "L'Ours et l'Abbesse," or in the exquisite pastorals of "La Clarté de Vie," his verse is marked by peculiar suppleness and rhythmic undulation.

Viele-Griffin has for some years employed a trenchant prose style in defence of the moderns. Under his editorship, "Entretiens politiques et Littéraires," to which all the leading men of the party contributed, Paul Adam, the novelist; Henri de Regnier, the poet; Gustave Kahn, Émile Verhaeren, Bernard Lazare, became a valuable ally of the cause of symbolist innovation.

We may perhaps discern something of Viele-Griffin's poetic intention in the dedications of the two volumes of his collected poems—the first,, "Au fin parler de France," the second, "Au printemps de Touraine." The beauties of the pristine *langue d'oil*, the virtues of a French speech not yet Latinized, are very dear to the new brotherhood of French poetry; and Viele-Griffin especially delights in the *roucoulades* and *chansons de gestes* of the ancient *trouvers* which have lent a setting to his modern thought.

Our country has of late years sent to Paris many students of painting who have quickly won distinction, but M. Viele-Griffin is probably the first American who has been termed "of all French poets of the present day the poet who is mostly truly French." M. A. V.

VIELES

The little town of Schaghticoke in the upper Hudson Valley,
once the hunting ground of the Schaatkook Indians, was turned
over to settlers by the Corporation and Council at Albany about
1708. Thither came Louwis Viele from Schenectady, with money
to purchase land received from the sale of his father's lands in
that place. Thither came his cousin Debora Viele and her husband, Daniel Kettlehuyn. Then Johannes de Wandelaer, Jr.,
son of the Deacon of Albany, joined the little settlement, together
with Harmen Knickerbocker and Marten Delamont, who had
married a Viele, and a few others.

It will be seen how Schaghticoke has become even more than
Schenectady the early home of the Vieles, or at least of the largest
branch—that of the descendants of Louwis Viele, "only surviving
son" of Pieter Cornelisen Viele and his wife Maria, the daughter
of the Huguenot, Frere. It is to mark the religious feeling in
the family that the list of those who were Deacons and Elders in
the Dutch church there is subjoined. The record begins with the
existing church lists.

1763. Nov. 1, Deacon Jacob Viele.
1765, Oct. 14, Elder Hugo Viele.
1769. Oct. 20, Elder Peter Viele.
1772. Feb. 6, Elder Jacob Viele.
1776. Dec. 2, Elder Jacob Viele.
1779. Jan. 1, Deacon Abraham Viele.
1782. Dec. 12, Elder Jacob Viele.
1783. Deacon Abraham Viele.
1783. Deacon Peter Viele.
1793 Deacon Lewis Viele.
1794. Deacon Teunis Viele.
1795. Elder Abraham Viele.
1796. Deacon Simon Viele.
1795. Elder Abraham Viele.
1796. Deacon Simon Viele.
1797. Elder Abraham Viele.
1797. Nov., Elder Ludovicus Viele.
1798. Deacon Simon Viele.

INDEX